Bryce Bevill's TOTAL FOCUS of Character, Academy, Discipline, and Faith

Copyright © 2008 Bryce K. Bevill
All rights reserved.
ISBN: 1-4196-9441-3
ISBN-13: 978-1419694417

BRYCE K. BEVILL

BRYCE BEVILL'S TOTAL FOCUS OF CHARACTER, ACADEMY, DISCIPLINE, AND FAITH
LIFE LESSONS FOR TOMORROW'S YOUTH TODAY

2008

Bryce Bevill's TOTAL FOCUS of Character, Academy, Discipline, and Faith

Chapter One -
OF CHARACTER   1

    Character Building for Students and Athletes   4
    Shaping Our Youth   6
    Solidifying Their Character   7
    No Easy Way Out   9
    Trying to Get a Rep   12
    Character, Deviance & Violence in Schools   14
    Parents & Educators   17
    On Teachers   21
    Family   24
    Family Breakdown   25
    Role Models   26
    Mentors   28
    Stages of Development   30
    Progression   31
    Responsibility   36
    Conflicting Worlds   37
    Temporary Feelings of
        Despair—"Kids, we did say TEMPORARY"   38
    Identity Crises   41
    Communication   42
    The Ride to and from Home   44
    It Takes A Village   46
    The Villagers Weigh In: Are Youth Ready?   46

Chapter Two-
ADMINISTRATION, FACULTY & ATHLETICS　　51

 Concerned Parents　　54
 On Child-Rearing and Discipline　　56
 Mixing Academics & Athletics　　59
 Interdisciplinary Learning　　61
 Health & Wellness　　62
 By Any Means Necessary—
  Help Them Further Their Education　　63
 Coaching　　64

 State Of School Athletics　　68
 Secondary School Programs　　70
 Health & Sports　　71

 The Value of Sport in Society　　72
 Relationships　　72
 Reciprocal Benefit　　75
 Adversity Training　　76

Chapter Three
FAITH & DISCIPLINE　　81

 Faith In Action　　84
 Parent/Child/Community Faith　　87
 Religion & School　　90
 Power of Prayer　　92

 The Art of Self-Mastery　　92
 Self-Discipline　　94
 Self-Management　　95

When Students Ask, "Why Are We Doing This?"	98
The Parents Again	99
Peak Performance	101
Getting There	102
Firepower vs. Willpower	103

Chapter Four
ENDANGERED SPECIES — 107

In Case You Haven't Heard:	109
By SAKINA PITTS: Public School Educator	109
ENDANGERED SPECIES	
The Marginalization and Devastation of African American Males	111
SOCIAL CONTEXT: Where Bad Seems Good	112
ENVIRONMENTAL CONTEXT:	
The Blame Game	116
Adult Examples	118
ADD—Absent Dad Disorder	119
Disappearing Male Muscle	120
INSTITUTIONAL CONTEXT:	
Institutionalized Segregation	122
Institutional Intervention	124
The McNamara/DeMatha Lesson	125
The Level Playing Field	127
Athletics and the Black Male	128

Special Report: ON THE POSITIVE SIDE — 133

Same as it Ever Was?	135

To the Future and Beyond	136
Academic Parity = From At-Risk to "At-Promise"	137
Self and Peers—Positive & Healthy	138
Technology	141
K-16 Schooling	141
Distress vs. "Eustress"	143
Re-Entering Society	146
On Point for College	148
Alternatives of Higher Ed	151
Combating School Violence	153
Career Exploration	154
Networking	154

A Summation   173

Among the many family and friends of both Bryce Bevill and Bubba Grimes, we want to thank you for the support and encouragement you've extended us over the years. We just hope that in some small way this book will inspire, uplift, and empower those of you who have children, grandchildren, godchildren, mentees, nieces and nephews.

From the bottom of our hearts, we'd also like to extend our gratitude to the hundreds of thousands of teachers, principals, deans, coaches and staff in our nation's schools for your contributions to helping tomorrow's youth, today.

INTRODUCTION
By A. Jerome Espree
www.soulofsyracuse.com

Points of View

As young children, some of us older folks remember when we took grandma's big old mason jars outside in the summertime to hunt and catch bumblebees, wasps, yellow-jackets, and blackjacks. We'd crop a few flowers from the bushes and put them in the bottom of the jar. Then punch holes in the cap so they could get air.

We'd creep up on the unsuspecting insects that landed on a bush and cover them with the jar until they jumped on the flowers in the jar. We'd then cover the top and twist the cap shut. As soon as the insects realized they were trapped, they would fly into the sides of the glass jar and eventually fly upward to the holes in the cap with the idea that they somehow could get through it.

After dozens of attempts, the insects would slowly give up trying to make it out of the jar...Their willpower was drained out of them after so many attempts to break through the glass walls and slightly opened ceilings. After a few days, they'd lie in a nearly catatonic state with barely enough energy to breathe and eat. Then the shocker!!!

We would open the top of the jar and let it sit outside for days and those six-legged winged creatures would never ever try to fly or crawl out. In essence, their willpower would be so broken that they would essentially give up to the point where we couldn't free them if we tried.

Three Strikes

Many young men in American society are literally born with three strikes against them. African Descendant males in this nation have (1) historically been marginalized, oppressed, or suppressed to the extent some of them fail to achieve because they are conditioned to achieve failure. Their skin color alone is their first strike.

The second strike is many of them are raised in inner-city or predominantly black neighborhoods. Most of the schools lack the pedagogical resources to prepare them to compete in any other arena except…that's right, third strike: Athletics.

African-American boys from inner-city or black neighborhoods who bet their lives on achieving their American dream of professional sports are often ill-prepared to enter the workforce. Thus, we can all look around and see an absence of black males in the upper-echelons of private business, education, and industry compared to the numbers of black males in the lower-echelons of menial 9-to-5 jobs, unemployment, and of course prison.

Somehow, some way, black males must struggle to overcome the same kind of psychological self-disintegration experienced by those honeybees in order to reach higher levels of achievement in private business, education, and industry.

"It's Time to Dance"

Roosevelt "Rick" Wright, a college professor at Syracuse University once told one of our authors that his presence on that campus was in his words "a walking miracle." He told the young man from Washington DC that American society never made universal provisions for the development and empowerment of the African-Descendant male. Dr. Wright encouraged the young man to strive for greatness at whatever cost. In his invincible words, he said, "Young fella, it's time to dance!"

Compare & Contrast

There are a number of glaring differences and distinct similarities between our two authors. Bevill was born in Miami, Florida and was raised in PG County Maryland. He attended the nationally renowned DeMatha High School in Hyattsville, Maryland and Syracuse University.

Bubba was born in the original Chocolate City section of Washington, D.C. known as Southeast Washington. He had the privilege of attending a DC public school, PG County public school, and a private Catholic High School—Bishop McNamara—in Forestville, Maryland. Bubba too attended Syracuse University.

Upon finishing college, Bryce competed for a roster spot with the NFL Detroit Lions and played for the Saskatchewan Roughriders and the Winnipeg Blue Bombers, both of the Canadian Football League. He was nominated for defensive rookie of the year. He was a starting defensive back in the Grey Cup championship game and intercepted the stellar quarterback—Doug Flutie—in that game.

Bubba never seized the opportunity to pursue professional football. Football itself was never enough for him. The game was too limiting for his broad mental interests. In college he helped to found the first student-run multicultural organization on the Syracuse University campus. It was a remarkable endeavor with

Franklin Redd, a former high school quarterback and college sprinter (who was later elected the first African-American student government president at Syracuse University). It was also during this time that Bubba got his first glimpse into the realities of "real life" that is usually hidden to star athletes.

By stepping outside of the security of the college football program, Bubba saw how politics, sex, religion, race, and socioeconomics affected how decisions are made in every aspect of life. His passion for politics and business began to grow and he exercised those interests for two decades in the Syracuse area. However, GOD also called him to devote more of his life to education. Scared out of his mind because of the impending financial mediocrity of the teaching profession, Bubba did everything in his power to run away from that calling; eventually running into his own "Jonah"-like experience.

Bevill and Bubba's paths were on a collision course without any forewarning. Bevill played for Syracuse in the early 1990's. Bubba played for the Orange in the early 1980's. There was a huge demographic and attitudinal shift in the Syracuse football program within that decade. Consequently Bevill's experiences were markedly different from Bubba's.

An Historical Context

Avatus Stone of Washington DC was the first black quarterback at Syracuse and created quite a firestorm within their college community in the 1950's because of the perception that he was a little too comfortable with Caucasian females on campus (Freeman, p. 82). Stone had limited opportunity to show his skills at Syracuse. As he faded from the college football scene, there was another more enigmatic "baller" from Long Island by way of St. Simons Island Georgia that was emerging as the one who would change the course of history at Syracuse: His name was JIM BROWN.

As soon as Brown hit the campus, he was warned to not give people the same perception Stone gave them. Brown did exactly the opposite. Not only did he give the same impression, he flaunted his penchant for the females for everybody to see as he drove up the hill to Archbold stadium on game day in a drop top red Pontiac Bonneville (and a blond-haired co-ed in the passenger seat). The biggest difference between Brown and everybody else was that Brown was virtually unstoppable on the football field and extremely independent off of it so he could do things that the rest of us could not.

In Brown's final days of college, Syracuse recruited another black football player from the opposite side of New York State with a very different demeanor. Elmira, New York brought the Orange "The Express": ERNIE DAVIS.

Davis was the first black football player to win the Heisman trophy. He was the antithesis of Brown. Davis was unassuming and cooperative on campus. He avoided controversy as Brown ran to it. Ever popular, Davis became the standard for black male athletes at Syracuse but never lived long enough to see the effects of his legacy. Davis died of leukemia shortly after leaving Syracuse.

Arguably, Brown became the greatest player to ever play the game.

The historical context of Syracuse football would have a profound effect on Bevill and Bubba, and many other black athletes but few knew it at the time they were there.

The landmark sociological shift for Syracuse University football came in 1970. Greg Allen, John Lobon, and several other brothers fell into conflict with their coaches and the University in general as they sought fairness, equity and opportunity for black athletes and all students on campus. Martin Luther King had been gunned down a few years earlier and these guys' eyes were opened to the hypocrisy and inequity of America and on that college campus.

Ultimately the nine guys, known affectionately now as the Syracuse "8", boycotted the Syracuse University football team and were summarily dismissed from the athletic program. Shortly after, Syracuse employed an unspoken rule of "6." Every freshman football class for the next 15 years would have no more than six black football players. Whether by design or default, it was the norm.

Upon Arrival

Coming from the Chocolate City, Bubba never let loose of his soul-inspired, "P-Funk-induced" DC roots. His arrival was a rarity because after Stone, Syracuse Football wasn't too keen on bringing in brothers from the DC area. Frankly, it was roughly 25 years later when the program enticed Archbishop Carroll's David Brooks away from Boston College (BC was getting all the Carroll boys) to sign with the Orange. However, it was a long-legged speedster from PG County Maryland's Largo High School who signaled the migration of stellar DC area boys to Syracuse to play football (Dave Bing opened things up for basketball many years earlier). Eric Wade ("Swade") was the marquee football player from the DC area who opened the doors for others, including Bubba, to sign with the Orange.

Another monumental event occurred to cement the interest of DC area football players toward Syracuse. For twelve years, Washington Redskins' head football coach George Allen traded away his Redskins' first round draft picks for older and more established veterans. Upon his departure, the Redskins drafted Syracuse University's Art Monk which gave Syracuse Football a staunch presence in the DC area for the next decade plus as Monk revolutionized the wide receiver position in the NFL.

When Bubba arrived at Syracuse hoping to join the legion of legendary running backs, Larry Csonka, Brown, Davis, Floyd Little, Jim Nance, Joe Morris, and Art Baker, he unconsciously termed his freshman class "The Black Six." The Black Six was a 1970's movie featuring some of the greatest names in professional football, "Mean" Joe Greene, Carl Eller, Mercury Morris, Lem Barney, Gene Washington, and Willie Lanier. For Bubba, there was no better tribute or honor than to name his freshman brothers after those gladiators.

But Syracuse University and the football program was struggling to re-gain its earlier prominence and Bubba experienced the toil, trauma and pangs of the Orange's renaissance. It was difficult for him to fit into the culture, lunacy, and intensity of Division One Football as he tried to create a football identity on the college scene. The Orange program did turn around under Coach Dick MacPherson and Bubba enjoyed the fruits of the rise. However, another McPherson "tore the roof off the sucker" and put the Orange back in show biz.

Donald G. McPherson—Donnie Mac as we know and love him—was the first black quarterback to ever star for the Orange. Donnie, a skinny kid from where else…Long Island, was a phenomenal athlete and turned out to be an even better person. On his recruiting trip, during a pickup basketball game at legendary Manley Fieldhouse, Donnie displayed his athletic energy. With Bubba guarding him in hot pursuit, Donnie took off on a fast break and leaped from the middle of the foul lane with Bubba draped on his back and flushed the ball inside the rim. The players went wild and Bubba was reminded of that day for the next 25 years. Before he drew big applause in the Carrier Dome in football, Donnie announced his arrival that wintry afternoon in Manley Fieldhouse on the basketball court.

The football team played basketball at Manley all of the time. It was also a cool place to watch the Orange basketball team play until, riding a 50 plus home game winning streak, the Orange lost to those dreaded Georgetown Hoyas. On that evening, Hoya coach John Thompson drew first blood by ending the winning streak on the final game to ever be played there and grabbing the PA microphone to announce: "Manley Fieldhouse is officially closed!"

After Donnie dunked on Bubba, Bubba took the time to get to know the young fellow from Long Island. He told Bubba he was a high school quarterback. When asked what position he thought he'd play at Syracuse, Donnie said, "quarterback." After Bubba picked himself off of the floor damn near unconscious from laughter, he realized that this fool was serious.

Bubba explained to Donnie that it was a far reach for him to expect to play QB for the Orange but maybe GOD will part the seas for him. Well GOD did, and Donnie ended his career as runner-up to the Heisman trophy his senior season and a perfect 11-0 record in 1987.

By the time Bevill arrived at Syracuse, the Orange had recruited and played Donnie, Marvin Graves, Kevin Mason and other black players named Womack and Lowery at the QB position. Interestingly, the Orange football team during that period also changed from a team that was 30% African American to nearly 60% black by Bevill's freshman class. The racial demographic shift on the football team was part of Syracuse's evolution by the time he arrived.

Bubba came to a Syracuse team with a perennial losing record and 2 wins, 9 losses his freshman season. Before that, Bubba's high school team had 1 win and 9 losses his freshman year. By his senior season, both his high school and college teams were either bowl bound or playing for championships.

An Unlikely Merge

The comparisons of the environments in which Bevill and Bubba played football and basketball are very significant to their personal and professional outlook. Where Bevill is accustomed to joining established teams of championship caliber, he only knows how to win at every level. Bubba, however, has joined football and basketball teams of abysmal quality and helped build them to a respectable or championship level. Consequently, Bubba has the patience and tolerance to endure the growth curve and ignorance of the untrained mind. Bevill, on the other hand, has less patience to put up with the manipulation and excuses that go with a losing mentality.

Bevill went to DeMatha and played for a high school that competed for the championship in football and basketball almost every year before his arrival and every year he was there. Bevill arrived at Syracuse on a program that had secured a string of major bowl appearances and an outside chance of a national title before he put on a pair of cleats for them.

What Now?

Due to their experiences, Bevill is now an educator and head varsity football coach. He knows how to step in to a situation and help propel it to new heights. Bubba, however, has never coached at a school in his life. He knows about the commitment, agony and loss assumed with the coaching profession in general and wouldn't wish it on his worst enemy. Bevill has tremendous analytical skill and has shown the ability to coach his teams to victory against seemingly insurmountable odds. He is somewhat reserved and keeps his eyes set on his mission to build championship-caliber football programs because that is what he knows. More like a military strategist and field general, Bevill is short on words, long on character, and deep in his principles. He has an unshakeable and impenetrable demeanor which is a great attribute for a leader preparing troops for battle.

Bubba on the other hand is far more political and outspoken. An incessant writer and profound speaker, he studies the architecture and barometer of every situation. With a gift of clairvoyance and intuition—born of his Cherokee Native American heritage—Bubba shows a deep sensitivity for his fellow man and is willing and able to sit down at a table with people from every walk of life. In a 1985 article for the student body newspaper (The Daily Orange), his mother described him as being able to talk well to the young and old, male and female, black and white.

According to Bevill and Bubba, contrasts among people can cause resistance and closed-mindedness but can also create incredible opportunities when given half a chance. They've learned from experience that one man's funk is another man's flavor and anything is how one looks at it.

It is based upon their experiences and perspectives that Bubba and Bryce began their working relationship. After hours of conversation they both realized that they had the same kind of life story played out at different times and in different venues. Their commonalities—an insatiable appetite for championship quality and a limitless interest in young people—gave them the opportunity and willpower to work through their differences to collaborate on projects that help develop the character, academy, discipline and faith of youth; a cause which they are devoutly committed. It is Bryce Bevill's **TOTAL FOCUS** of youth development that drives them forward when the manipulation of politics, the selfishness of humanity, and the hypocrisy of academia interfere with that cause.

Their willpower to help redirect youth, especially African-American males, is what keeps them from a similar fate to that of our honeybees.

PREFACE

In The Beginning

One evening at a young lad's home in the Washington, DC area, a physical fight breaks out between his parents. After listening to the arguments and observing the hostility, this 13 year old boy realizes that he can't take it anymore and heads out the front door. As his parents are screaming now at him, he continues to walk with the thought that he was never going to return.

It was no ordinary (depending on the judge) household because the boy's biological father expired from a stroke a few years earlier. His 7 year old younger brother died in a tragic accident a few months after. There was drugs and violence in and around the house all of the time.

His disjointed and disconcerted home life left him with a feeling of helplessness. A little later the young man started stealing, fighting, cutting school and harassing teachers; eventually moving up to joining gangs and selling dope.

Across Inner-City, USA, there are many of the same types of stories to share. However, this particular story describes the life and times of Bryce K. Bevill.

He never returned to his mother's home but found refuge with an older brother, Gary A. Mack. Gary gave Bryce the first opportunity to learn how a responsible man conducts himself in society. He had the keys to the house, learned to drive and went on his first date while living with Gary. Bryce also developed an affection for a man who he now calls "Dad."

"Dad" was his basketball coach who was told by his uncle to take hold of Bevill right then and there and never let him go. He invested countless hours in that young man and showed him what it meant to operate with integrity, character, discipline, and faith.

Coach Tony Watkins saved Bevill's life and helped him find meaning in it. He was a "Man of Standard" who mentored Bevill and tried to attend every important event of his life, from Boys Club to professional football.

But Bevill learned an even more valuable lesson from Coach Watkins because he was not the only kid that "Dad" put under his wing. "Dad" had a group of 15 boys and some of them made real bad life choices.

"Come, follow me and I will make you fishers of men"
Matthew 4:19 KJV

Since that time period, Bryce has dedicated himself to the lives and times of other youngsters. He is working with youth to help them to develop positive character, discipline, integrity, academy, and faith. Bryce has realized that the struggle to raise the standard of youth is ripe with confusion, hypocrisy, politics and resistance. He also understands that "persistence kills resistance"; so on he persists.

This humble literary offering from Bryce Bevill and Bubba Grimes only scratches the surface of the challenges and difficulties working with tomorrow's youth today. There are multiple natural and man-made forces that work for and against youth who are trying to remain positive and fruitful. Here, we look deep into just a few of them.

CHAPTER ONE
Of CHARACTER

"And thou shalt do that which is right and good in the sight of the LORD; that it may be well with thee, and that thou mayest go in and possess the good land which the LORD sware unto thy fathers"
Deuteronomy 6:18 KJV

A young man, just turning 15, is allowed to attend his first house party with his high school friends. It's Friday afternoon and he can barely sit at his desk in school as he watches the clock on the wall. His teacher is slowly going through the day's lesson and he feels like it is taking forever.

The bell rings and students are talking about tonight's bangin' party at every locker he passes. As he hops the bus, he checks his cell phone which registers nearly 20 text messages about the same party.

Once home, he tears through his chores, wolfs down his dinner, and hops into the shower; full of anticipation and wonderment about the night's possibilities. After a grueling 90 minutes of changing clothes and trying on different colognes, he kisses Mom and high-fives Dad as he jumps in the backseat of his best friends' car. Along the way he reflects on his parents' warnings: "No alcohol, no drugs, be home by 1:00am."

In the car, one of his boys pulls a bottle from a brown paper bag, takes a swallow and passes it around the car. When his turn comes up, he shakes his head and passes it back. By now he is the butt of their jokes. He shrugs it off, remembers his parents' words, and focuses on the party.

At the party, more than a few people have pulled brown bags from under their jackets and a few more are rotating into the bathroom for the occasional hits on a "joint." But the boy is cool, he's no fool and just continues to dance to the music and "say no" to the booze and weed.

As he is sitting in a corner chair, he suddenly spots a young lady moving across the dance floor that he didn't have the nerve to speak to at school. As she nears, he reaches out his hand and asks for a dance. Without missing a beat, she snatched him to his feet and danced all up in his face.

Thirty minutes later, she grabs his hand and walks him to the next room to refresh on some punch and chips. She shows a strong interest in him and as the conversation flows, he grows more comfortable with her and thinks that maybe this could be the start of something.

She walks him out back and a few of her friends are standing around the deck, passing the brown paper bag. She takes it from a girlfriend and chugs some of it down, and then passes it to him. He freezes, wondering if this is the moment he shows he's cool and downs some brew or not, risking the opportunity to spend more time with her. He takes the bag, thinks about it real hard and then...

Character Building for Students and Athletes

"Train up a child in the way he should go, and when he is old, he will not depart from it"

Proverbs 22:6 KJV

Young people in our nation are confronted with all kinds of challenges and opportunities today. Youngsters are far more connected today with the rest of the world than any time in history. Modern conveniences such as the World Wide Web have made it easier for today's youth to connect to others all over the world in no time flat. Because of that, youth have options that their parents could only fantasize about. How they view themselves and the worlds around them directly affect how they respond to those challenges and opportunities. How they view themselves and the worlds around them is directly affected by their relationships with many different people with whom they interact.

Popular settings like MySpace and Facebook give youth the ability to connect to others across the U.S. and world. If not properly managed, these internet portals will become a major distraction and crutch for a young girl or boy. They will interfere with their school work, complicate their friendships, and aggravate the "beejeebers" out of their parents. As well, they entice youth with spectacular fantasy and daydreaming; which can be dangerous to their underdeveloped psyche.

These portals also provide academic and professional information that might prove very useful; linking youth with others who have blazed a trail before them in high school, college, and the working world. They are ideal for networking with people and businesses that can help youngsters to find hidden college/career opportunities.

Not to be outdone by MySpace, video game companies have created intoxicating games that titillate the minds and emotions of young players. Many sites offer the chance to play chess, checkers, etc. with people all over the world. These kinds of games can have recreational and soothing effects on youth when they are bored or troubled. However, there are other games that give sensational violent and sexual images likely to blow a young person's mind. At some point they can become more desensitized toward it and develop a twisted view of their response to society's darker side.

In a free society like ours, youth make decisions everyday about whether they will obey their parents' directions or ignore them. Naturally speaking, as children grow older, it is common for them to depend less on their parents' input and more on others outside of their home. In the neighborhood or at school, youth have a chance to test their character on a daily basis. Each day they have to decide where and how they will invest their energies in school, at home, and in the streets. Their foundation of character is perhaps the strongest force in helping them to decide how they will act and react to the things and people they encounter.

Shaping Our Youth
A youngster's character shall provide a filter for any decision he/she has to make and be revealed to others wherever they go. Youngsters with strong, unflappable character will aim to do the right thing all the time; especially when NO ONE is watching. This is the best measure of their character and helps them to see themselves from the inside-out.

Parents, educators and coaches should consider focusing foremost on forming their character while raising our youngest students and student-athletes. Any activity on the field, in the classroom, and in the neighborhood provides an opportunity for youth to learn life-long lessons that influence their moral behavior. Character formation/development is not a one-time task; it is an all-the-time task. It happens when youth are sitting in class, doing chores at home, and playing with friends in the local park. Numerous things will block, intercept, and challenge the character development of our young; which is a main reason why parents definitely want to help direct their children's habits and activities.

Youth have an amazing ability to understand right from wrong but receive mixed messages from society. Youth are exposed to tons of "misinformation" in politics, sensationalism from college and professional sports, and folktales from peers and adults. Although youth have an inner sense of right from wrong, they often observe others who seem to do the wrong thing yet prosper and even be rewarded for their achievements. Naturally this makes them wonder "Why shouldn't I?" take shortcuts, cheat and lie or steal since so many others are doing it and getting what they want in life.

Daily they see drug dealers living the high life and politicians and businesspeople who pay a fine after breaking the law and continue business as usual. Classmates cheat on exams, skip school, and curse their teachers and are still promoted to the next grade level.

As character formation takes place in the home, church, school and neighborhood, everyone surrounding them participates (even if they don't realize it) in a youth's development. The saying, "It takes a village to raise a child" certainly rings true because anyone can help shape a youngster's mind and heart. Parents, friends, and teachers offer advice and direction to our youth daily and aids in their personal development. In general, adults help youth to establish a foundation of character early and often. In both formal and informal ways, adults can role model and teach youth how to make good choices in private and public.

Solidifying Their Character

As youth internalize positive teachings, they may want to record character goals on paper or in a diary/journal as a sort of positive reminder during tough times. Goals, for example, that remind youth 1) about their A-B-C's (action, behavior, consequences), 2) to respect those in authority, and 3) to whom much is given, much is required. Adults may want to promote those character goals in creative and entertaining ways like role playing in class and family Q & A's at home. Parents and children can learn and practice the ideals of "moral reasoning" by teaching kids how to respond positively to various situations they may encounter.

Adults in a young person's life will not intentionally tell them to do something that will cause them harm (but there are some and youngsters should have limited contact with them). However, it is the youth's responsibility to hear, accept and utilize the good counsel he/she receives as they get older and reject anything that does not improve their lives and the lives of others around them. Parents, together or separately, should strive to send consistent messages to their children about their moral and ethical decisions.

A youngster's character shall provide a filter for any decision he/she has to make and be revealed to others wherever they go. Youngsters with strong, unflappable character will aim to do the right thing all the time; especially when NO ONE is watching. This is the best measure of their character and helps them to see themselves from the inside-out.

In many old school homes, they teach "The Momma" rule (would Mother approve of what you are doing right now?)

There are many things that all of us say and do that we wouldn't do in front of our parents. Those are probably good things to just not do at all.

Character is both an internal foundation and external exhibition (what's inside influences outside and vice versa). Other people will always form a good or bad impression of a student based on how he/she conducts him/herself. Internal character influences decision-making as well as reveals the moral fiber of a person. Internal character also affects external behavior. Our internal character is always under attack and has to be strengthened on a constant basis, but not everyone will celebrate the youth who show positive internal character. For some youngsters, internal moral character is a burden because family/friends ridicule or put them down; and others encourage them to do the wrong thing or take shortcuts.

No Easy Way Out

"The soul of the sluggard desireth, and hath nothing; but the soul of the diligent shall be made fat"
                                                                    Proverbs 13:4 KJV

One of those "shortcuts" gets a lot of students into a lot of trouble everyday. In the world of academia, there is a never-ending problem of children cheating on assignments, test, and quizzes. Quite a temptation, cheating can rescue a student from a poor grade and even increase his popularity among some peers. Since most young students are not working jobs or managing finances, their behavior in school is the window into their character. Therefore, cheating in school is probably the most visible test of character for our youth. Sometimes the students who have the highest academic and professional goals are the ones who do the most cheating. Recently, a handful of high school graduates from a ritzy suburb in upstate New York were charged with manipulating high school computers and changing grades (http://www.syracuse.com, Nov. 2007). If this is true, regardless of the reasons, their actions are hurtful to everyone associated with their school.

Whenever faced with the temptation to cheat, youth must learn not to give in to that desire. The effects of it can be devastating to the student and community. From the moment it is discovered by others, a student is never looked upon the same again. Cheating is a decision and action that can spill over into just about any aspect of a person's life because it is habit-forming (Johnson, p. 26). In other places, the desire to cheat can lead to bad relationships, thievery, and slothfulness. Cheating habits formed in childhood don't always disappear by adulthood. A few years ago, the Superintendent of a school district in New York State was arrested for shoplifting at a store in her district. Allegedly, she stuffed her pockets, clothes, and bags with store merchandise until caught by a store clerk. Apparently, she'd been shoplifting for quite some time at the same store; chances are she'd been "boosting" since she was young.

Youth can find good character advice/counsel in books, magazines, television shows, and even music. There are all sorts of magazine and internet articles for students to read which reveal how their action and behavior leads to good or bad consequences. Good character can be built on the playing field and in the neighborhood as youth learn to practice hard and play hard when the rules are the same for everybody. Although these are ideal places to grow good character, they can also present obstacles to good character formation. Good character can be lost at a party, lost under the bleachers, in the classroom and in a chat room. There is an old wise saying, "Garbage In/Garbage Out." When youth consume garbage with their eyes and ears, they have a greater chance of internalizing that garbage and damaging their character. Every place they travel has both positive and negative attributes. Youth will participate in things which appeal most to their positive or negative internal character.

Character is shaped by the many positive people in a young person's life but good counsel must be exercised by the youth themselves. Children are taught how to strengthen their positive character by the very same people, places and things which help shape their soul. By taking good care of their bodies, mind and spirit, youth can strengthen their good character and build the necessary "internal armor" to fight off negative influences. By feeding their bodies the right kinds of foods at the appropriate times, attending spiritual worship, and reading books/listening to music that promotes healthy habits, youth will have a better chance to build "character muscle" to carry them through most situations. In doing so, the eventual temptation to lie, cheat, and steal finds little room to grow in a youth's heart. It is ever-important for aspiring student-athletes more than others to build and strengthen their character on a continual basis because it will surely get tested early and often.

Character can be shaped during any negative or positive experience. By incident or accident, a person's character grows every time he/she has to make a decision and live with a consequence. For example, whenever a student-athlete meets his/her academic or athletic goals, they have an opportunity to strengthen their character by remaining humble, continuing to work, and acknowledging those who've helped them in some way. By the same token, when the same student-athlete fails to achieve his/her goal, they can build character by evaluating their progress, modifying their approach, and continuing to work. In either situation, continuous pouting, gloating, or cheating does little to strengthen character. In other words, win or lose, there is something to gain whether they like it or not.

BRYCE K. BEVILL

Trying to Get a Rep

"Even a child is known by his doings; whether his work be pure, and whether it be right"

Proverbs 20:11 KJV

How a student-athlete demonstrates his/her character will help to create their "reputation." One definition of reputation is how that person's character is viewed by others based on past behavior, comments, and achievements (Johnson, p. 106). In the adult world, reputation is viewed as the most important aspect of social, professional and civic relationships. Adults decide daily if they are going to utilize a service or engage another person in any way based on what others say about them. Reputations, as many of us have been warned, can take lifetimes to develop and a few bad moments to destroy. Reputations are built and reflected in job evaluations, financial credit histories, academic grades, and in the company one keeps. It is vital for every student to learn at an early age that they have to protect their reputation. Once a reputation is destroyed, it is hard to recover, especially in today's information age.

Recently, many of us have read the stories about entertainers, politicians and athletes destroying their reputations while making horrendous decisions. Whether it's lying about doing drugs or steroids, embezzling money, or spying on an opponent, the reputation of such perpetrators can be severely scarred. One such example, Michael Vick of the NFL was charged with animal cruelty, conspiracy to commit interstate illegal gambling, and other violations. Reports show that Mr. Vick is losing hundreds of millions of dollars in future money-making endeavors. The reason: No one in their right mind wants to sell their product or service through someone who is believed to be a menace to society. Vick may never be able to re-establish his good name in society.

In speaking with many high profile college coaches, it is apparent that they are becoming very aware of how to conduct themselves publicly in order to avoid tarnishing their reputation too. One coach remarked that he refuses to even drink a beer in a public place because he's concerned that his picture would appear on the internet. Unfair and suffocating as that might seem, it is today's reality and tomorrow's norm and aspiring young professionals must accept the responsibility of conducting themselves in a smart, self-controlled manner in public. In 2006, the head football coach at Arkansas was embroiled in controversy as the residents of the state petitioned to have his emails and phone records available to the public. Needless to say, he quit his position a year later and ended a rather embarrassing moment in NCAA football history.

Undoubtedly, the actions of some of us adults set a poor example for the youth who look to us for guidance. Some of us still believe in "do as I say, not as I do" as an effective way to raise our children. Many of us want to conduct ourselves as if our actions shouldn't affect youth around us. In a commercial some years ago, the NBA's Charles Barkley said that he is not a role model. He urged youngsters to turn to their parents to become their role models. He was absolutely correct...and incorrect too.

Parents are the initial role models for young people but parental influence diminishes as youth establish relationships outside of the home with peers, teachers, coaches, etc. Parents are still the parents, but let's face it: The majority of students spend more of their waking time away from their parents than they do with their parents. Eventually, the influence of others carries increasing weight as youngsters naturally establish independence from their parents.

Our young student-athletes are building or destroying their personal reputations from as early as grade school. As money gets tighter for us all and students come to our colleges from all over the world, more high schools, colleges and employers are reviewing the behavioral history of candidates as much as their academic pedigrees. Educators and managers will turn a negative eye toward potential employees with a troubled past; even if the problems date back to high school.

By no means do we suggest that mistakes and poor decisions won't happen because they will and they do. In the earlier example, do you think the young man turned down that beer or chugged it to impress the girl? You bet ya! He chugged...*but still didn't get the girl.*

In most instances, youngsters will have the opportunity to recover their good reputation and society will forgive the mistakes of their youth. However, it may require some work and time to right the wrongs and change a negative image into a positive one. With every fabric of their being, youngsters should make the effort to walk the straight and narrow and abide by the rules and regulations in their home, school, and playgrounds. Whenever they stray from that, they need to make every effort as soon as possible to get back on the right track. It is easier said than done as most adults already know.

When youngsters fail to demonstrate quality character, not only is it not the end of the world for them, it often requires more character to repair a damaged reputation or rebuild trust with parents or teachers, and peers.

Character, Deviance & Violence in Schools

Approximately 15% of junior and senior high school students have unexcused absences from school daily (Stephens, 1997).

Youth deviant behavior has always been a major issue in American schools. From truancy to violence, youth's anti-social and negative behavior is a disruptive and costly aspect of youth development.

Truancy is a huge problem for schools as students skip classes and are inexplicably absent from school. It is an age-old problem (Gullat & Lemoine, 1997) in need of modern day solutions (McCray, 2006). Students who don't feel a sense of belongingness to their school will look for outside support and may decide to "play hooky" from school to spend time with their friends and acquaintances. It is an alarming statistic among upper class students: Approximately 15% of junior and senior high school students have unexcused absences from school daily (Stephens, 1997).

Students missing at least 30 hours of classroom time are in jeopardy of failing school (McCrary, 2007). Another problem is that their refusal to regularly attend school eventually leads to juvenile delinquency, drug/alcohol use (Baker, Sigmon, & Nugent, 2001; Strickland, 1999), diminishing educational accomplishments, and a lifetime of social/professional problems (McCray, 2006). If a youth thinks his/her world is difficult to endure while they are in school, they haven't seen anything yet because it only gets harder as they get older when they've refused to invest in their own education while they were young. Unfortunately, truancy not only affects the student but extends to their family and community as well (McCray, 2006). Truancy is a definite precursor to escalating deviant behavior among youth; leading to social mischief and criminal violence.

According to the Children's Defense Fund an American youth is arrested for a violent crime every five minutes (Edelman 1995) and is killed by guns every two hours

(Webber, 1997). More youngsters were killed by guns between 1979—1991 than all of the Americans killed in the Vietnam War (Edelman, 1995) and our kids are 15 times more likely to be killed by gunfire than children in countries like Northern Ireland (Webber, 1997).

More than half of the people arrested for murder in the U.S. in 1991 (Wilson & Howell, 1993) were under twenty-five years of age. Children have been committing increasingly more violent acts and at younger ages over the past 30 years (Walker, Colvin, & Ramsey, 1995), with the majority of the violence against other youngsters (Webber, 1997).

Violence against and by children has reached "public health crisis proportions" according to the United States Advisory Board on Child Abuse. The Office of Juvenile Justice and Delinquency Prevention (Wilson & Howell, 1993) has asked for "unprecedented" national support to curtail the rise in juvenile violence and family disintegration (Webber, 1997). The juvenile violence problem is very costly in terms of incarceration, treatment and loss of productivity; not to mention a continuous embarrassment to one of the world's most progressive and powerful nations that is an international leader in human rights and human development (Webber, 1997).

Truancy and juvenile violence has landed many youth in prison. Many of them under 18 years old (Snyder & Sickmund, 1999) have been prosecuted and sentenced as adults (Kupchik, 2007). Many states have increased their number of adult jails and have ceased to invest in juvenile detention facilities; thus pressuring the courts to prosecute more youth as adults because of limited space in youth correctional facilities and juvenile group homes (Kupchik, 2007).

Of course, introducing more youth into adult prison populations (Austin et al., 2000; Bishop a Frazier, 2000;

National Institute of Corrections, 1995) will create practical problems in how to manage children in a confined space with adults (Kupchik, 2007). Youth in adult prisons are far more likely to be physically assaulted and receive less therapeutic help than those in youth correctional facilities (Kupchik, 2007). The outcome of this situation is that youth in adult prisons become hardened, desensitized, and more likely to return to jail in the future.

Parents & Educators

How students react to stressors and pressures in their school environment is directly linked to how they view the school's organization, safety and security, and teaching motives. Any school program that addresses the potential for violence in their school will focus on some of the basic violence prevention, drug/alcohol usage, vagrancy and truancy and unique school population traits to help create a positive school climate (Peterson & Skiba, 2001). An individual school's location and population demographics will cause schools to address issues that may not be a problem at other schools even within the same district.

A comprehensive approach to school violence generally includes methods to prevent violence, such as identify and intervene when students are having difficulty of any type, and respond effectively when inappropriate behaviors surface to keep it from escalating (Peterson & Skiba, 2001).

When parents and educators team up to establish mutual goals between them, there is a greater chance for the students to experience a healthy and consistent learning environment in school and at home. When other community stakeholders get involved with the school there is a greater chance for the learning environment to extend to the greater community. By fostering a spirit of community service and volunteering, more local residents will support the school's objectives (Peterson & Skiba, 2001). This will have a positive impact on the labor pool which local employers can draw from and it will affect neighborhood stability which translates into appreciating property values, etc. Whenever a family relocates to a new area, the first question parents ask is how are the schools? The second question they ask is how are the neighborhoods? Few parents want to raise or expose their children to imploding schools and trashy neighborhoods.

Securing parental and community involvement in a school is much more than a notion. Some school leaders must spend time and energy pursuing parents and other community stakeholders with little to show for it in the beginning. But if they have the willpower to continue they will eventually seep into the consciousness of parents and neighbors to draw more of them into the fold. Overall student success and improved school attendance are outcomes of consistent parental involvement. Parental involvement instills pride and enthusiasm in school programs that enrich the entire student body (Peterson & Skiba, 2001).

"Children, obey your parents in the LORD: for this is right. Honour they father and mother; which is the first commandment with promise; that it may be well with thee, and thou mayest live long on the earth"

Ephesians 6:1-3 KJV

How do parents build an effective value structure within their children? Every parent worth their salt wants the best for their children. Parents can't change the world their children live in, but can teach them how to handle themselves in it. There are many different ways for parents to teach and train children to respond to their value system. Most of us already know how because our teachers, parents, coaches, etc. did it with us. However, many adults just don't believe that the old parenting structures they were raised by will work today because kids are so different and society has changed so much and there are so few neighborhoods.

So what! Everything has not changed.

Babies still need to be kept warm in the winter and cool in the summer. They still need their diapers changed and someone to feed them. Toddlers still need to feel safe and be watched over so they aren't in danger from themselves or others. Adolescents still experience hormonal changes and need to feel more independent. Children still learn through their five senses: touch, taste, smell, audio and video. Certain things have never nor will ever change as long as humans inhabit this earth.

Guardians and teachers are still teaching children through their five senses. Children still take cues from the people around them and parents/educators are probably their primary role models. Those cues will help shape their character and fortitude but one visible difference between parents of today and parents of yesterday is that parents of today are raising children in a world with many more choices. The variety of choices and exposure can confuse children about what is proper and improper behavior in a given situation. Back in the day, as they say, we ate what was cooked, watched what was on, and wore what we had. Children had fewer opportunities to veer off the narrow path because their whereabouts and activities were more structured and monitored by adults.

There is absolutely nothing wrong with children having more choices today than they had yesterday. It is a sign of human progress. The choices itself is not where the problem lies. The problem lies with children who are not rooted enough in how to make those choices based on a positive long-term value structure. Parents who teach and train their value structure to children consistently and with consequences will raise children with a stronger likelihood to use good character responses anywhere they go.

The variety of choices available to youth today makes it harder for parents and teachers to keep a child's full attention. Many parents are frustrated because too much of their teaching and training time is replaced by the television and video/internet games their children are playing. Here's a noble idea: Turn the television off and lock away the video games. It's probably best to do that when they are very young before they get too dependent on them and they rise up and strike you!

Many parents and teachers are passively training children instead of actively engaging them. When children are not actively engaged, they wander; physically and mentally. As they wander, there is no telling where they will end up unless they have a strong value structure ingrained in their minds and hearts. Teachers have an awesome responsibility to guide children in their academic growth and character development. For educators to be effective in their teaching and training of students, they have to clarify expectations of and aspirations for their students. Inconsistent and confusing messages about the importance of education and character can make school harder on children than it should be (Graham, 1998).

Parents and educators know that children learn from the behavior of the adults around them. Out of respect, a student and child may not say it, but may feel that too many of the adults around them are hypocritical in their behavior. It's not only what we say that matters but what we do that matters more. Parents and educators must strain to remain consistent and exemplary even when it pains us. Parents and educators must set rules because rules enable people to live together and focus on their goals (Johnson, p. 110) and rules are vital to students' ethics and actions. Students are forever breaking the rules but their misbehavior offers "teachable moments" that are priceless.

Unfortunately, many classroom teachers use a "refer-and-remove" philosophy for non-compliant students. Most often this happens because teachers are unable to relate to a diverse student body or lack the training to assess student behavior and fail to link the possible causes for such behavior. More glaringly, many classroom teachers are simply unable to develop student-specific teaching techniques to support student success for each individual student (Gable, et al, 2005).

On Teachers

Teacher competencies vary widely depending on their personal and professional experience. Their experience and exposure affect how they respond to any one of those hundreds of times each day when teachers and students have momentary tensions between them (Gable, et al, 2005). By the same token, students have their own collection of experiences and exposure which shape the way they respond to situations. Many students are unable to handle personal problems and can not navigate difficult social situations (Gable, et al, 2005). Naturally it interferes with their ability to select an appropriate response to tough situations and lands them into more trouble with their teachers.

When students can't relate to the teacher or feels the teacher can't teach them it is just a matter of time before they show disrespectful and disruptive behavior; further alienating them from not only their current classroom teacher but all of the other teachers who hear about them in the faculty lounge. At that point there are stronger and more negative consequences (Gable, et al, 2005) for non-compliant behavior and the 'labeling" of those students as having emotional/behavioral disorder is just a stroke of the pen away.

For those unfortunate young souls who are intent on controlling the classroom and manipulating their peers and teachers, swift and pronounced intervention strategies are the way to go (Gable, et al, 2005). Those are times when the guidance counselor, psychologist, and deans of discipline should be utilized when teachers detect an arising problem. When teachers sense that students are trying to wrestle control of the classroom, they have to act swiftly and may want to refer them to another adult in the school building to intervene.

Students are far less inclined to disrupt their classrooms when the teachers give them clear and consistent expectations with numerous opportunities to engage and respond in class (Gable, et al, 2005). It also helps when students feel that teachers are treating and responding to students the same way across the board; even if the teacher uses hardboiled techniques. If a teacher is hard-nosed and inflexible with some, they should be that way with all so each knows the same pathway to success in their class. One example, NFL Hall of Famer Willie Davis once said of legendary football coach Vince Lombardi that he treated all of his players alike: *Like Dogs!* He demanded the most out of his players and addressed the superstars the same way he talked to the third-stringers; and many of them loved him for it. Lombardi's Green Bay Packers were one of the most successful franchises in the history of modern day sports. Many of us have encountered a few teachers with the same style but if they mete out discipline evenhandedly to all students they will gain their respect and allegiance.

Some educators are suggesting that schools become more active in addressing the moral and civic values that are reflective of our civilized society. If a spirit of moral cooperation and mutual respect is felt throughout a school, it will help to de-escalate potential problems between students. Whenever students interpret the intentions of others as a lack of personal respect and moral regard, it can trigger a variety of unwanted responses ranging from insensitive and inflammatory verbal remarks and internet "blasts" to physically aggressive confrontation (Gable, et al, 2005). If students perceive that their classmates have an interest in and commitment to maintaining positive moral character they are more likely to seek constructive alternative ways to handle their conflicts. To promote moral character among their student population, many schools teach character education as a "curriculum" and organizational function throughout the school community. Some of these character development goals include:

- Promotion and development of mutual respect and cooperation (improves feelings of self-worth and promotes positive behavior toward others)
- Growth of "moral agency"—the ability to sense and react with moral principles (moral reasoning about doing the right thing)
- Creation of a community based on equity and fairness with a support system inside and outside of the classroom—extend acts of kindness, courtesy, and build trust (Peterson & Skiba, 2001).

Successful school environments with fewer incidences of violence are able to take students away from their preoccupation with self. It is not an easy thing to do especially with students hailing from non-traditional or broken homes (Freeman, et al, 2003). However an ideal way to help students to "get outside of themselves" is through the arts.

The arts help students to analyze and act out roles and work cooperatively with others. The arts in school train students to think externally and restrain internally in order to produce and perform well.

It is virtually impossible to work well with others when a student has a lack of emotional control. Teachers can use creative drama theatre to help students to create and role play stories and situations that promote their social literacy and maturity.

Family

Everyone recognizes the impact family has on shaping a young person's character. Family members can influence children in a number of different directions. Most often, children take their cues from their parents first, then their siblings as they get older. Down the road, children are increasingly influenced by extended family members depending on the depth and frequency of their interaction.

In order to build a strong character base within children, family dynamics have to play a large role in the process. Whether headed by two parents or one, the biological family is the basis for a youth's character development throughout life. Where there is inconsistency and breakdown of the family foundation, character development can suffer. Everything starts at home but may end elsewhere. Where youth go and who they go with will have a direct impact on where they end. A youngster starts the race at a deficit when he/she lives in a home with a lack of family structure.

Family Breakdown

"For where envying and strife is, there is confusion and every evil work"

James 3:16 KJV

Educators are apt to take into account the effects of separation and divorce on children because so many of their lives are altered by parental breakup. Divorce causes many changes in youths' lives, especially in their interaction and contact with parents. It also affects how well youth adapt to academic and social environments (Leon, 2003). Divorce may be very hard on young children but a supportive family and home environment can reduce the risk of potential problems in the future (Leon, 2003).

The younger the children the more they feel responsible for their parents' divorce. Younger children will have more anxiety and "fear of abandonment" than older children (Leon, 2003). Without purposeful intervention from parents, educators, and therapists, parental divorce can scar young children for a lifetime. Successful intervention should consider a youth's early life experiences, current family dynamics, and stage of development (puberty, adolescence, young adult).

Many youth have a very difficult time period after divorce but will adjust well enough along the way to accomplish appropriate tasks at various stages of development. As they realize divorce is probably a permanent situation, they may experience "sad or unpleasant emotions" (Leon, 2003) that are strong, yet temporary.

In fact, if a child's parents divorce while they're in grade school, it may have little effect on their progress in high school and beyond. Unfortunately, some youth never adapt successfully to life after their parents' divorce (Leon, 2003).

When parents separate or divorce, if they are able to maintain a working partnership it would be beneficial to their children; even if they do not have a good personal relationship between them. The only way to keep a successful partnership between them is to take their personal feelings toward one another out of the equation. This will allow them to focus on and better address the needs of their children.

Parents should never hold their ex-spouse in contempt for wanting to spend time with their children. Parents must be careful not to use their children as a "hammer" to spite their ex-spouse. Children should never get caught in the middle of disagreements or bitterness between parents because it further confuses the children, especially when they are young. Parents will often look for a way to experience fulfillment or wholeness after a breakup but using the children against the ex-spouse may not be the ideal way to fill those voids.

Although it may not look like it early on, progress will take place if parents don't try to squash each other but try to find a way to include their ex-spouse in important school and family events. Parents should try to never miss important dates like birthdays, holidays, etc. when they live in town. As much as possible, be courteous to ex-spouse's family members to reduce friction.

Role Models

One of the biggest influences on a young person's character is the role models they choose to copy. Sometimes they copy the characteristics of others without even realizing it. In today's society there is much debate about the artists, athletes and actors that our children see on television everyday. These entertainers blaze across the television screen and capture youths' attention. Are they or should they be role models? When they do something wrong, do they stop being role models? In essence, the argument is probably moot. The more visible and celebrated our entertainers, the more youth aspire to follow in their footsteps.

Children often emulate the behaviors of others they watch, whether it's on television or in real life. Anyone can portray a role that is "modeled" by a young person. Some of those roles are villainous, heroic, athletic, or academic. Role models can be family members or friends. They can be different persons they see on television or hear on the radio. They can be strangers, and teachers. They don't have to be famous or even very popular. As long as they appeal to a youth's value system, youth may imitate some aspect of the individual's persona.

Do not be mistaken, all youngsters have different value systems. They may place a value to a particular style in one arena and completely abandon it in another. They may value a particular friend when it's time to play chess but would never ever consider picking that person for their team in neighborhood pickup games. They may hang around one group of peers at school and a totally different group at the park. In studying and learning our children, we can figure out how to better influence their decision-making by observing who and how they interact in different settings. Like it or not, some of these people are their role models within different settings.

These friends and family, along with those they see on television, are a legion of "role models" that affect youngsters' behavior and influence their character. It is impossible for parents to gage and understand the value or impact these individuals have in their children's minds. Although some parents try by hovering over their children's every move, there is simply no way for parents to filter every person that comes into their child's lives. This is why it is so important to solidify a value structure within children at the earliest ages possible to help them to become self-sufficient in making good choices. Their value structure affects their choices and their choices reflect their character and their character builds or destroys their reputation.

Mentors

Many youngsters pattern themselves after someone they hold in high regard. They also respond well to older, more experienced persons who have an interest in them and offer guidance in some way. These people, commonly known as mentors, are essential in every youth's life. Good mentors can have a huge impact on the character development of our youth. Mentors come in all shapes sizes and colors and are regularly chosen by the youths themselves, unless they are provided by an institution. Mentors are fathers, uncles, aunts, teachers, coaches, barbers, hairstylists and neighbors. Mentors can play a variety of roles in children's lives. For young males when a father is not in the picture, mentors can play a fatherly role. Young and impressionable men and women shape their relationships around adults with whom they can identify.
Mentors can shape the way a child views the world and in most cases are just as influential as parents. Whether a mentor relationship develops through a formally arranged mentorship or by fate, mentors can profoundly affect a youngster's behavior and perspectives on friends, family, school and sports.

Bevill's brother and coach, for example, mentored him in the responsibilities of becoming a man. They prepared him to be accountable for his actions. They prodded him while he was a little fella to engage in healthy activities and avoid drinking/smoking and drugs. They taught him by words and deed to do the right things in order for good things to happen to him. Obviously they couldn't guarantee that his righteous living would protect him from all danger, but their teachings could/would motivate him to get back on track when things went awry. Consistent contact with mentors who serve as role models and can identify with the youth can facilitate their "socially appropriate behavior and reduce delinquent behavior" by youth (Keating et al 2002). Studies suggest that without intense contact, mentoring is not effective.

Although mentoring can be a time-consuming endeavor, it positively affects both the mentee and the mentor. Mentees have a "trusted friend" with whom to learn new experiences and gain new skills, observe appropriate behavior modeled by the mentor, "experience multiple interactions with individuals of different backgrounds", and learn to "practice the expected norms" of their environments (Barton-Arwod & Jolivette, 2000).

Depending on the environment and challenges youth face, there are different types and degrees of mentoring required in helping them navigate through society. For example, youth, black or white, from higher socioeconomic households may not need mentoring that is geared to at-risk youth but may need mentoring regarding their career/professional development and moral choice. Youth from higher socioeconomic homes rarely struggle with gun-violence in their neighborhoods but may have difficulty choosing career paths or avoiding driving daddy's car under the influence of alcohol. In either situation, mentors can advise youth on their decisions and teach them how to correct their mistakes.

Stages of Development

Children develop through different life stages. They grow from infants to toddlers to pupils to teenagers to young adults. However the "adolescent" phase of development is perhaps the most peculiar.

Many parents fear the onset of the adolescent stage of youth development. A youngster's character runs through a battery of trials and tests during this phase. Like it or not, children are going to become adolescents and experience rapid or profound physical, psychological and emotional change. Many parents find it hard to let go of the student's childhood but adolescence is inevitable (Johnson, p.16). The concept of adolescence comes from the "Latin word adolescere- to grow up" (Johnson, p.15). During this phase of youth development, children begin to see themselves and the outside world differently than before.

Adolescents may discover that their relationships with others also begin to change; especially the relationships with those in authority. Adolescence is a difficult period to live "comfortably with parents and teachers" (Johnson, p.15). It is during this phase of youth development that children can be more rebellious and outspoken or just the opposite, conforming and introverted. As children "grow from childhood to adulthood-that is, through adolescence"—they are less dependent upon their parents and more receptive to the whims of their peers; this can be a very difficult "life center" shift for parents to accept (Johnson, p.15).

Adolescents commonly experience internal changes that are both noticeable and hidden. They have all "sorts of feelings of body and mind, many of them having to do with sex" (Johnson, p. 16). These feelings can be incremental, incidental or persistent but are "puzzling to the student, parent and teacher" (Johnson, p. 16). There are times when these feelings cause problematic behavior at home or in school. Although many parents recognize it as adolescent behavior, it doesn't make it any easier for the parent or teacher to handle.

To better equip youth for the onset of adolescence, youth must be conditioned to understand and accept the *ABC's* (Action-Behavior-Consequences) of life during the toddler and pupil stages. From a very early age, youngsters can tell when they delight or disappoint others with their behavior and therefore can determine if they are doing the right thing based on the response of others. Still, somewhere along the way, youngsters may learn not to take ownership for their actions.

However, accepting responsibility for one's actions is an important part of growing up. Again, youngsters do not automatically gain a sense of responsibility and should be taught how to be accountable. As they practice it, they can strengthen their profile and reputation among their peers and adults. When they accept blame and admit wrongdoing, parents and teachers may gain more trust and admiration for the student (Johnson, p. 25).

Progression

Although most of us think that adolescents are not ready to discuss "real-life" issues, they are far more ready to address mature themes than we know. Much of society is unclear of what is expected of adolescents (Kaplan p. 9-10) and therefore are uncertain about when to talk about mature issues. Society expects them to be mature enough to exercise self-restraint but deals with them as if they are not responsible enough to function without adult supervision. As a matter of fact, independent functioning is what they will do in college and in the real world. Chronologically and cognitively speaking, is there much difference between a 17 year old in high school and an 18 year old in college? Those of us who've worked at least 10 years with adolescents in high school and college already know that the only visible difference between them is their options.

As children grow through their life stages, when they become adolescents they should be "more able to (self-) impose structure and better assemble separate bits of information" (Kaplan, p.8). Adolescents are far more able than in previous life stages to "gain the ability to imagine possibilities not currently present in daily experiences, fantasize of present and future choices, and blend facts and thoughts and arrive at conclusions" (Kaplan, p.8).

Their blossoming self-awareness can be noticed in how they think critically about things like their own grooming and dress. They are more able to crystallize and articulate their thoughts and feelings too. They are more able to "think critically even about their own thinking" (Kaplan, p.8). Adolescents are habitually "uncertain of what to do and how to do it as they move from schoolchildren with all of their needs met by parents and teachers to becoming adults with self-understanding; ultimately developing the capacity to accept full responsibility for their own actions", (Kaplan, p.9). It is helpful when parents, teachers, mentors, older siblings and friends help adolescents to clarify their concerns and identify possible solutions (Kaplan, p.10); but devastating when those very people constantly offer conflicting guidance. When expectations are clear to students, "they can take one step and make one small decision at a time"

(Kaplan, p. 11). Guidance counselors, psychologists, social workers and student deans can fluidly assist in this process.

Adult leaders can be of significant help to the development of youth if we incorporate methods of "trial and error which can move them closer by steps, half-steps and occasional missteps" (Kaplan, p.10). It can be paralyzing for an adolescent to perceive his/her actions in school and at home as "all-or-nothing, now-or-never propositions" (Kaplan, p.10). Whenever behavioral expectations are cloudy or unknown, "young people feel pressure to act without understanding how or where or why; discomfort and anxiety result" (Kaplan, p. 10). By teaching the same behavioral expectations to youth in class, on the field, and in community service, those expectations become clearer and more concrete.

Adolescents who broaden their exposure and opportunities through athletic competition and artistic expression will find that co-curricular activities aid in their self-awareness and self-actualization. Through these activities, they can "focus on their own interests and abilities and select those academic or extra-curricular experiences that will broaden and deepen them" (Kaplan, p.10). Because their concepts about education and achievement develop within home, school and social contexts (Bempechat, 2004) extra-curricular activities can bridge relationships between those seemingly separate domains. Extra-curricular activities also give adolescents some freedom from their parents and siblings.

Adolescents need to develop "independence from their parents, learn decision-making skills and the personal mastery to act on their own and live with the consequences" (Kaplan, p.13). Adolescents may be uncertain about these goals and be "dependent on parents and other adult leaders because they privately lack the confidence and skills" (Kaplan, p.14).

Through those co-curricular activities, their peer group begins to define what is normal as they move away from their parents (Kaplan, p. 14); which is why it is important for them to choose the right peer group.

There are estimates that surmise that teens suffer three times as much stress as 15 years ago. Today's youngsters are growing up in very fluid environments with drastic economic and social changes (Kaplan, p. 1). Thirty years ago it was unheard of for a 15 year old to drive to school in a luxury Cadillac unless he was singing on stage with his four brothers. Thirty years ago we did not have microwaves and cell phones. We had to go out of the house to see a movie and daydreaming was the closest we came to a videotape. All of these things make it tough on youth to balance schoolwork, jobs, dating, and other activities (Kaplan, p.2)

Today's youth are more sexually aware, politically indifferent, depressed, and fearful than teens of yesteryear. Statistically, seventy-five percent fear AIDS, forty percent considered suicide and experienced violence in school and half deal with peer pressure to have sex. At the same time, fewer teens are in constant rebellion against adults and experience less of an emotional roller-coaster (Kaplan, p. 2). Today's teens are noticeably more energetic and intense and are more adept at critical thought. Teens are becoming more at ease with their person as they gain self-awareness and confidence (Kaplan, p. 3)

We've all come to know adolescence as a period of multiple changes and developments (Kaplan, p. 4). Some of those changes are physical and some are psychological. Perhaps the most lasting changes in adolescence occur at their "perceptual" level. It is during adolescence that youth turn a critical or analytical eye toward the adults in their lives (Kaplan, p.5). This can be a great source of conflict between parents and children as children also start to set expectations for their parents' behavior.

During the period of adolescence, youth establish more autonomy and deeper relationships with the opposite sex too. At this time, youth go from fantasizing about building relationships to assessing their own interests (Kaplan, p. 5) so they can better formulate those relationships.

Parent-child relationships, no matter how strong, begin to take a new form as adolescents migrate to resources and supplies outside of their parents or home. In fact, heavy parental involvement could be frowned upon by peers and educators as an inordinate attachment to a child. At this stage of development, youth "begin to find a vocational direction" (Kaplan, p. 6) that affects their decisions regarding time and tasks.

Adolescents who experience drastic psychological changes are the toughest for academic institutions to handle; which is one of the reasons that the prison institution warehouses so many of them. In adolescence, our children get bigger, faster, and stronger in a hurry. For some, it is hard to sit still in classrooms for 6 hours a day and be cool the whole time. Yet that is what we are telling them to do and it contradicts what their internal physiology is telling them to do.

Adolescents become more temperamental and enigmatic as their thinking and behaving patterns don't work as well for them (Kaplan, p. 7). They think "radically different" from the way they thought as a young child. Plus, poor eating and sleeping habits increase their irritability and tension (Kaplan, p. 8). As a result, educators may grow intolerant of their lack of maturity and poor responses and issue multiple detentions which in effect, ask them to sit still for another hour or two after school or on weekends (no doubt about it, that'll teach them).

Academic institutions have to function in a civil and orderly environment with young customers who are having a naturally hard time keeping still and quiet. We tell them not to chew gum or bite their nails but for many of them that is how they compensate for their nervous tension and anxiety. At the same time, declining school budgets mean fewer P.E. classes. To effectively manage adolescents in school, educators must develop programs within their schools that address nutrition, exercise, and emotional growth. Easier said than done as the federal, state, and collegiate academic mandates and expectations continue to rise, leaving little time for psychosocial intervention.

Responsibility

Character improves as youth learn to be accountable for their actions. Part of being a responsible youth is obeying parents' wishes in the home. One of the ways parents can give a sense of responsibility to youth is by assigning chores around the house. For many youngsters, chores are viewed as a burden and interruption to their play or rest. When asked to do chores, youth should not "dwaddle" or make excuses. They should "do chores on schedule or explain why they didn't" (Johnson, p. 31). Depending on the time and level of parental trust, youth may ask for an alternative time or method to complete a chore.

Many youth perceive chores as a bore or punishment but they are quite the contrary. There is something very liberating and satisfying about willfully accepting a task and seeing it through to completion. In terms of youth development in general, chores teach youth how to take care of themselves and the gifts around them. GOD does not guarantee a cozy home and backyard for everybody and these gifts must be cared for.

It is a beautiful thing to see young persons accept responsibility by taking care of their home and school environments.

Chores also give the parents insight into the attitude and determination of their children. They can use chores as a teaching and training tool for character development and self-discipline.

There are varying schools of thought about the value and utility of parents assigning chores. Some believe that youth should be active participants in deciding what and when they should contribute to the household. Others believe that children don't need to make those kinds of choices while they are living under a parent's roof. Some also think that chores should or should not be used punitively. Every parent must decide how to employ chores for every child in their home and be consistent with their expectations, evaluation, reward, and punishment.

Conflicting Worlds

Never in history has the life of an American student been as complex as it is today. Mass transportation and mass communication has given students insight and access to many different worlds in a very short time relative to just 20 years ago; and the world will only get smaller and faster. As we speak, a multinational communication consortium is wiring undersea cable infrastructure from the U.S. to China (soulofsyracuse.com, Nov. 2007).

For tomorrow's students, it is important for them to crystallize (see clearly) the worlds around them and develop a sense of gravity (grounding) within those worlds if they are expected to take ownership of their lives. "Students have one life-divided into several parts—home, school, friends, family, church and teams—" (Johnson, p. 33). There are times when those lives conflict and compete against each other. When this happens, youth may be torn or confused and parents can feel exasperated.

Temporary Feelings of Despair—*"Kids, we did say TEMPORARY"*

A Gallup Poll revealed that nearly 70% of 16- to 24-year-olds think their parents lived in a better world and that it will be even worse for their children. Most people don't believe they can trust government or other people and many youngsters see little hope for tomorrow (Stephens, 1997).

These feelings of being overwhelmed and not in control can lead to depressive and even suicidal/homicidal thoughts. Suicide, as we've come to realize, is an unalterable, permanent solution to a set of temporary problems. No matter how bleak things may look to someone, every problem and ill-feeling associated with those problems are temporary. When experiencing suicidal thoughts, youth should try as early as possible to talk it out with someone they trust or a professional at their school. Youth should seek help immediately even if they don't feel they need it.

Another more common youthful reaction to life's pressures is rebellion. Rebellion of itself has opened doors and changed lives and can be a valuable tool for change. Rebellion has its place in society and can create positive social change where needed…home is perhaps not one of those places. History and the present teach us that rebellion can be purposeful, admirable, and heroic; but is almost always harmful and destructive at home and in school with parents and teachers. It's not unnatural to wish to rebel occasionally but if those feelings persist, youth probably could use some help; and so too probably their parents (Johnson, p.104).

Parents can have a very difficult time with the fragmented lives of their children because they too have one life in many parts: home, job, community, and friends. The pressures and intensity of maintaining balance in these different domains can be enormous for parents. Those parents who've been taught and trained when they were kids to recognize and manage themselves in these different domains should be better equipped to do it as adults. Establishing a set of rules for the child and sets of rules for oneself can help parents to maintain the proper daily flow of their life's activities; "Rules, systems, and order, in a sense, "give us an excuse not to think" (Johnson, p. 111), but to comply.

Parents, teachers and coaches should keep a trained eye on how young student-athletes manage their different lives. Due to the time commitments and "insulation" of student-athletes, many never recognize that they have to function in these different domains and experience debilitating shock when they are held accountable for their actions or lack of action within these different worlds. Many of these young men and women "feel messed up inside their heads or feel they are no good at anything…some feel that nobody really loves or understands them or can possibly understand how miserable they are" (Johnson, p. 130) as they try to navigate through every aspect of a seemingly disjointed life.

Student-athletes, especially, often bring a competitive mentality into each world that they function. To compete means to "work hard to accomplish a set of goals" and it also means to "strive against someone else as a rival in an effort to win" (Johnson, p. 33). Student-athletes must be trained to avoid competing against parents and teachers unless it is during a prescribed game with identifiable and agreed upon prizes. Special events like faculty versus team soccer games can be a great time of mutual competition and regard between adults in authority and the youth they serve. Those are unique times when they can share in the sportsmanship of competition without it becoming a conflict that hinders a student's progress. Students should never compete with teachers for "control of the class" (Johnson, p. 33) or with parents for control of the home.

"A soft answer turneth away wrath: but grievous words stir up anger"

Proverbs 15:1 KJV

However, in human dynamics, conflict inevitably arises and becomes either a stumbling block or stepping stone to healthy student-adult relations. When conflict arises, there are a few practical steps any of us can use to handle conflict appropriately. They include:

- Define the problem—Talk and write it out until the problem is defined and agreed upon
- Brainstorm solutions—Talk and write out potential solutions and
- Evaluate the solutions
- Agree on a solution—Keep the mutually agreeable ones
- Commit yourself to trying the solution
- Meet again and discuss how the solution is working (Johnson, p. 55)

When in doubt or unable to agree to a process, it is probably best to seek outside help (mediation). It is hard sometimes for adults to accept mediation when dealing with disagreeable youth, but it's good to have it in the backup plan. A mediator can be a friend of the family, a trusted relative, pastor, or an educator at their school.

Astonishing as it may be, it is natural for youth and adults to have conflict. Youth may for a time period challenge the authority of the very hands that feed them, but when appropriately handled, those moments will assist in the youth's maturation. As humans playing different roles, "parents, teachers, teenagers—the difference in our ages sometimes can make it harder to live together. Mark Twain recognized this when he wrote, 'When I was a boy of 14 my father was so ignorant I could hardly stand to have the old man around. But when I got to be 21, I was astonished at how much he had learned in seven years'" (Johnson, p. 150).

Educators and parents must rear youth according to the youth's particular needs and progression. Regardless of how negatively adults may view tomorrow's youth, they often are a reflection of the society adults have created. A few thousand years ago, "Socrates, complained that young people lacked motivation, were stirred by wild music, and were generally irresponsible (sound familiar). It's inevitable that sometimes the fact that our parents and teachers were brought up in a different generation from ours creates a gap in understanding" (Johnson, p.150).

Identity Crises

Youth are forever trying to establish and project their identity; consciously or subconsciously. One of the gray areas for parents is in determining how much privacy their children should have to develop and protect their identity. Recently

Dr. William H. Cosby remarked in a television interview that parents should go through their children's rooms, computers, etc. to see what their kids are doing with their minds. It is a long standing debate about how much privacy a child should have in their own homes. Many feel that youth "have a right to (some) privacy, to (their) own private place, where (they) can go and do and think what (they) want as long as (they) are not disturbing anyone else" (Johnson, p. 151).

Again, this is where a child's character comes into play. If a parent views their child as honest and committed to their family values, the parent may be more willing to embrace their child's desire for his/her own private space and time.

Communication

Effective communication between parents, siblings and students is valuable to maintaining harmony in the household. Students can be frustrated by many different things and display those frustrations in many different ways. Adult-child relationships are rather sensitive in nature but it is necessary that all youth respect adults in authority. There will be times when a youngster feels he/she is being treated unfairly by a parent, teacher or coach. When this occurs, youth should not "let a feeling of unfairness fester and grow; it may lead to resentment or rebellion" (Johnson, p. 146) as well as running away from school, team, or home. Their verbal and non-verbal communication will frequently cause a rift between them and others in their home and classroom. Children who are taught and trained to communicate effectively within the guidelines of their home structure will experience less tension in their relationships with family members.

Some of the key components to effective communication in the home include:

- Scheduling time to have open verbal communication among family members (reserve that time for exploration, not judgment so everyone can be as open as possible)
- Schedule time for discussion of things that are of a more sensitive nature (everyone in the home should not be a part of those discussions)
- Set rules for exchange- listen until the other person stops talking, make notes, tape the conversations if necessary, no cursing or inflammatory remarks

During these family unit discussions, bear in mind that words can diffuse or ignite emotions even when that is not their intent (Johnson, p. 146). In summary, a lot of the very techniques we use to manage the workplace do work in the home.

Students who are under fire from parents to keep their rooms clean, get good grades, and appropriately socialize with peers may find it hard to express themselves as things are happening around them. They will subsequently vent their feelings during emotional outbursts or withdrawals. If a student is open and honest with their feelings (in a respectful way of course) others will know how they feel when they are feeling pressure. Schoolwork obviously can create the most tension in a child's day. When dealing with schoolwork, students should let others they live with know beforehand that they have a heavy workload on the horizon. They should also tell others in the home when their workload eases up a bit (Johnson, p. 146).

Additional sources of family frustration center on mutual family property such as the television. "Television- whether to watch it, when to watch it, the effects of watching it, who controls it- is one of the major causes of friction between parent and children," (Johnson, p. 143-144). When utilized effectively, television can be a valuable resource, providing information and insight into numerous things (Johnson p. 144). Television allows the consumer to engage shows that are informative, humorous, dramatic and horrific. Everyone in the home could have different tastes in television broadcasts but there is always a common program(s) that all family members like to watch (e.g. sports, reality programs). It may not be a bad idea to "spend some time talking about what TV programs the family will watch together" and when it's over, "no matter how great the temptation is to go on watching more TV, turn it off and discuss the program" (Johnson, p. 144); although your kids may think it's corny to do that.

It is estimated that the average high school graduate will spend "11,000 hours in the classroom and 18,000 hours watching TV" (Johnson, p. 144). "Homework must come first" (Johnson, p.145). Television can be used as a reward for getting school work completed

The Ride to and from Home

Many parents commute their children to school each day. Baby-boomers can remember a time when we walked several miles a day to get to school. School has become less of a regional and more of a career academic choice for parents. No longer do most of us "live in villages and near most of our friends and activities" (Johnson, p. 142). The ride to and from school can be chock full of stress for both parent and child. As parents fight through traffic to get their youngsters to and from school on time, they are managing their lives in the car by PDA, cell phone and GPS. The last thing a parent wants to see when they arrive at school is a frumpy-looking adolescent with a depressed-looking face and a poor progress report in hand.

Parents and children should develop mutual ground rules for the commute just like they establish ground rules in the home. The daily commute can be fruitful and enlightening if managed in a productive manner. Parents should plan for those conversations about why their child is not at the designated pick-up point on time, because it's going to happen. They also should plan for the discipline and poor test grade conversation as well, because it might happen. Parents should prepare for the boy-girl conversations too, because those talks probably need to happen. For the commute to and from school, here are a few suggestions to make it more productive:

- Agree on consequences for not being at the designated pick-up point on time
- Determine in advance if you want to have discussions about grades, assignments, social issues, and co-curricular activities in the car
- Determine in advance how much you want to discuss in front of siblings (especially younger ones) and car-poolers
- Agree on use of the DVD, CD, radio
- Have backup plans in case either are late for designated pick-up point and time
- Cell phones are a great tool but must be used within the rules of the school environment

It Takes A Village

For students and student-athletes to develop outstanding character, it requires the positive input and discretion of many human forces. From parents to coaches, adults have a prolonged effect on the moral foundation of youth. Through positive role-modeling and mentoring, any adult can have a hand in helping youth to learn to do the right things in the right way.

Society sets standards for youth and youth set standards for themselves. Sometimes those expectations can be confusing to youth, especially as they become more self-reliant with age and exposure.

When parents, pastors, teachers and coaches are consistent in their training, youth are far more likely to avoid the pitfalls of making bad character decisions...or at least have a greater likelihood to get back on the right track when they stumble.

The Villagers Weigh In: *Are Youth Ready?*

"Absolutely less and ill prepared. It is systemic and to some degree institutionalized. Teachers think that passing a young man or woman in their high school courses will open the doors for them down the road and ultimately they set them up for failure because they are ill prepared and they realize it; so more folks leave college not by their own doing but because they are academically ineligible."

K. O. Miles

The viewpoints of the villagers vary widely and the jury is still out. With the massive amounts of information available right at their fingertips, are youth more prepared for the real world today than they were 25 years ago? Kim Marshall, a businesswoman in the DC Metro area believes, "In some ways kids are more prepared because of technology, but in other ways no...Many teens today are not taught proper business etiquette and respect for elders like they were years ago."

It's that same technological progress that leads Erin Smith of Upstate New York to conclude youth today are more prepared. Smith notes there are more students "applying for and getting into college. The internet has allowed even the poorest youth to compete on a global level."

Carolyn Evans, business developer/entrepreneur is concerned because she feels, "Our youth are less prepared. They have unrealistic aspirations and an under-developed work ethic. The education that they receive in high school is geared toward getting them into college, but what about the kids who just aren't college material? Kids are not taught about the everyday things that they will face, like buying a house, credit, health issues, advocating for themselves, etc...AND JOHNNY STILL CAN"T READ AND WRITE!"

Kenneth Chase, law school graduate who has spent many hours in secondary school classrooms, adds that "Kids are NOT better prepared than in the past...one must differentiate between public and private—urban and suburban exposure. My experiences say teachers are trying to prepare youth to make a living instead of how to live."

Another villager anonymously offers a similar theme, "No way. Kids need to spend more time reading the newspaper and not just getting their daily dose of news from the TV news stations. If they read it only on the weekends, that's good enough."

Kenneth O. Miles, educator and former college-student athlete addresses the issue from a scholastic level: Kids today are "Absolutely less and ill prepared. It is systemic and to some degree institutionalized. Teachers think that passing a young man or woman in their high school courses will open the doors for them down the road and ultimately they set them up for failure because they are ill prepared and they realize it; so more folks leave college not by their own doing but because they are academically ineligible."

John Elmore, law firm partner and author, senses that "Youth 20 years ago were more independent. Back in the day it was expected that youth go to college and graduate in 4 years. Today youth go to college and expect to graduate in 6 or 7 years. Twenty years ago kids had innovative ways to make money. We did things like shovel snow, detail cars, paint houses, and throw parties. We also worked menial jobs for minimum wage."

In his inimitable style, Charles Gilbert who resides in the DC area too, comments, "Youth are more prepared exposure wise; less prepared to analyze, make a sound adult decision and process the potential consequences." Michael Smith, a life-long educator and developer of youth, suggests (similar to Gilbert) that youth are "academically, more prepared with better tools and greater knowledge on how to use them. But they are socially, less prepared. With the advent of the computer and the influence of it, we are developing a society of individuals of loners who only talk to people via machine."

Sharon Owens, former collegiate student-athlete and a strong advocate for education and student discipline ponders, "Unfortunately I have to say no. The minimum academic requirements imposed by government are not equipping our children (USA) to compete on a global level; especially when focusing on minority high school students. Among Black males in particular, this disparity is exponentially magnified."

Owens continues, "Unfortunately there is an every increasing divide between students who are at least meeting the minimum requirements to succeed in high school and graduate and those who are completely disconnected from the entire process and will not finish."

Joshua Brown, an articulate, deep-seeded young musical talent from Southeast Washington, DC emphatically and simply states that youth of today "are far less prepared for the world than 20 years ago."

CHAPTER TWO
ADMINISTRATION, FACULTY & ATHLETICS

You are an administrator in a public high school that does everything to make sure the building is safe and secure and the faculty and staff are able to meet the needs of the students. You also have a very positive presence in the local community as you sit on numerous boards and volunteer your time to worthwhile projects.

To capture the enthusiasm of the people you serve, you advertise the ideals and virtues of the school to the whole community. You promote sportsmanship, honesty, integrity, character, discipline and faith. Right about now you figured that everyone around you is buying in and then...Kapow! There is an all-out brawl at the homecoming basketball game that evening.

The next morning, while debriefing staff and students you discover, to your absolute amazement, that the white kids don't like the black kids; and neither one of them like the Hispanic kids nor understand the Asian kids. If that's not all, the "nerds" have been beating up the "jocks" in the bathroom and the jocks joined the "bullies" to counterattack the "nerds' but the cheerleaders backed up the "nerds' while the dance team stole the cheerleaders uniforms and burned them the night before homecoming.

Not to be outdone, the black faculty members think the white ones are insensitive and the white ones think the black ones are "entitled" and the gay ones feel they're disliked by the entire staff. You can handle most of that until the 11th graders tell you that their 9th grade English and math teachers hate the cheerleaders because they think they're "skanks" and the P.E. teachers all hate the athletes and are trying to fail them but most of all, the white teachers pick on the black kids and get them in trouble while the white kids never ever get into trouble.

The life of administrators and other school educators can be very challenging. But most of them do what they do because they love what they are doing and really wouldn't think of doing anything else. They are constantly trying to balance the values and aspirations of multicultural, complex school environments. They have to respond to the needs of students who live multiple lives in education, arts and athletics.

Concerned Parents

Concerned parents have a myriad of thoughts and beliefs about the roles and responsibilities of school personnel—from the Principal to the Lunch Aide. Many agree that the first job of school educators is to "educate" youth, followed by maintaining the safety and security of the school community, and creating a shared environment where every student can realize their full potential in the classroom and on the playing field.

Chris Moreland is a realtor in Upstate New York who has seen lots of changes in the quality of education in his hometown. Moreland wants to know that teachers are educating the students "with the curriculum that is written by the school board." He also prefers that teachers "institute good moral judgment" in their daily activities with students.

Moreland advocates to the administrators to make sure that their teachers are "doing their jobs." Moreland adds that coaches should educate the student-athletes about "sportsmanship, leadership and respect."

Mr. N'namdi Muhammad, a community activist and artist, believes teachers are here to help "cultivate the gifts and talents" of their students. School administrators, also according to N'namdi Muhammad, should make sure that everyone in a school is doing his/her job. He expects there to be adequate checks and balances to ensure that all children are meeting the school system standards.

N'namdi Muhammad wants coaches to 1) encourage youth to have the best experience in school and 2) make certain that everyone on their staff lives up to the standards of the school system.

Candidly speaking, Kim Marshall hopes teachers will get to know their students and advocate for their needs. She thinks teachers should study their students and get to know them to better educate them individually.

Marshall asks school administrators to get to know the kids as well, and provide a "back-up" in the event teachers are unable to reach their kids every time. She adds that administrators are to follow, enforce and educate others on the policies and programs implemented at the school.

On the other hand, Marshall has seen some administrators "take their roles too seriously" and institute rigorous discipline to the extent that youth do not feel comfortable around them. She likes to see school administrators maintain an "open door policy" for students as well as refer them to other support staff (guidance, deans, etc.) when they are unavailable.

Marshall concedes that coaches should play the role of mentor, educator, friend and even "big brother" to their young athletes. She feels that coaches have a unique opportunity to connect with youth because they interact with them outside of the classroom. Because most students enjoy being a part of the team or playing their chosen sport, they are more likely to listen to and follow the instructions of their coach in order for the coach to gain more insight into the student.

Kenneth Chase sounds off about school systems and educators by adding, "The educational system is now a business, not a place of learning.......half the people in high administrative positions either have never taught on the ground level or forgot what front line teachers are going through. Plus, I'd like to see every elected official spend at least 2 weeks as a teacher's assistant in a public school. Then MAYBE SOMETHING WILL CHANGE."

On Child-Rearing and Discipline

"For whom the LORD loveth he correcteth; even as a father the son in whom he delighteth"

Proverbs 3:12 KJV

There is "more than one way of skinning a cat" the old song from the stage-play "Perlie" with a young Sherman Hemsley goes. People have different views on how best to raise and discipline children in our society. Some like the "corporal punishment" style of discipline while others prefer the "new aged action-consequences" method. A parent in the Maryland area explains some of her perspective on child-rearing with an open monologue of her experiences. Pamela Chisley is the single parent of two children (one high school senior and one young adult):

"I am a single, divorced parent (mom) for the past 15 years. I have raised a daughter who is now a 22 year old young lady that has graduated from high school and is now attending college and let's add...without the baby drama! I also have a son who is now a 17 year old young man that is a senior in high school with plans to attend college."

"I feel that even though they are aware that at any time I could have and maybe would have taken the "Old School" method with them, I can say that for the most part I did not have to resort to that. I used other means to discipline them, like taking the things that meant something to them or not allowing them to do certain things that they wanted to do or not allowing them to go certain places that they wanted to go. We talked a lot about their behavior and how it affected me and us as a family and I was able to (reach) them that way."

"Now, don't get me wrong they weren't and aren't perfect kids, but I do count my blessings that I didn't and don't have the problems with them that some of my friends and other relatives have had with their kids even after having both parents in the same household. After the separation from their dad (my ex-husband) when my daughter was 8 years old and my son was 3 years old, I went through the time of feeling guilty about the separation so I allowed them to stretch the rubber band a little further than I would have before. Then reality set in and I knew that if I did not maintain control of them and the situation—not that they were out of control—then I would lose authority over them and the situation permanently."

"Bottom line, I was never beaten by my parents (because of course I was a GOOD GIRL). I don't feel that I would have been the one to beat my children. But, that does not say that they did not receive a spanking every now and then."

But don't mess around with Mr. Joshua Brown of the original Chocolate City (Washington D.C.). This parent of an infant son is having none of that newfangled discipline in his home:

"I do believe "old school" discipline is the way to go! I don't know when giving a child a spanking became child abuse. America is in a negative position today that could have a lot to do with the "Timeouts." Kids don't fear their parents one bit. I think all children should fear consequences, if they were to think about doing something wrong. Now kids see everything as a negotiation. They can talk their way out of trouble, or run away from home. Now some parents can become abusive when giving discipline. You have to use strong judgment to know when enough is enough. Parents fear the consequences they'll suffer if they even touch their children. Everyone is letting America raise their Kids."

Mr. Michael Smith, strength and conditioning coach/personal fitness trainer, contemplates:

"Very young children—need discipline in the old fashion way, i.e. underline a smack on the bottom over a diaper etc. (especially when dealing with dangerous behavior like touching a hot stove). I disagree with smacking the face, head or even the legs. But the bottom with a hand is fair game and if used properly can be an effective tool that won't be needed often. With regard to school age children, we often hear that the schools have a "no discipline" policy and children end up running amuck. This I believe can be corrected but in essence you also have to retrain parents into being parents instead of being their child's friend. A parent becomes a friend after the parenting has stopped about age 21 until then the child relies on the parent for guidance."

"My Dad did wear my butt out with a belt and I believe I grew up to be respectful of my elders, my peers and to a great extent even to the youth in listening to what they say. I have also maintained a very high level of discipline and determination to get things done and at the desired results that I want."

"As for in-school discipline, in-school suspensions and detentions should be held in either a classroom or the library (so they can still do their schoolwork). In addition, I'd like to see the parents in the school for the same period of time. Once you start affecting the family parents will start demanding greater discipline and respect from their children. Do this the first week of school and you'll get about three months worth of cooperation from the students because the students will pass the word and none of them will want their parents in school. Then the parents will talk to each other and may start reaching out to more of the students."

Mixing Academics & Athletics

Administration, faculty and staff in school buildings can be very territorial and somewhat non-supportive of programs and projects within their school that do not promote their individual areas of interest. This is one of the reasons why there is often a separation between athletics and academics inside schools. The divide exists in many schools and often at the detriment of the students they serve.

Many school personnel have mixed feelings toward athletes in their school. Some just cannot see the value of sports and feel it detracts from education. However, there are major benefits to the school community when all of the school employees collectively support and celebrate the achievements of their student-athletes. The school personnel who recognize the value of athletics in their school help to create an enthusiastic school environment. In those schools, athletics help to strengthen school spirit and connects students across racial, cultural and gender barriers; thus extending membership to all of the students and reducing feelings of worthlessness and loneliness (Terzian, 2004).

School sports are frequently covered by the local press with no effort by or cost to the school. It's free press. The administration must understand that all positive press is good for the school environment. Not only is the positive press good for the school community, it can help revitalize the surrounding neighborhoods as well. Youth/scholastic sports are rarely displayed in a negative light by the local press and keep the school or youth league's name in the public eye. As well, many youngsters who struggle with identity and self-esteem are encouraged and buoyed by reading about themselves and their teams in the local newspapers.

Not surprising however, many school officials dislike the attention given to student athletes and specific sports programs within their school. Sometimes when an educator is not a fan of a sport or dislikes how a community is enthralled with the sport, he/she will turn a blind eye and deaf ear to that sports program; and quite frankly will turn a deaf ear to some of the student-athletes involved in the sport. Such interaction with school faculty can have a negative effect on the student-athletes' educational achievements (Harrison et al, 2006). Students, all students, are seeking acceptance and validation from the adults in the building. Whenever the administration, faculty and staff outwardly and privately displays interest in and celebration of their student-athletes, the student- athletes may be more receptive in class and more responsive to the interests of others.

It is vital to the development and well-being of student-athletes at every level to feel the support and endowment of their adult school leaders. Without such support, youngsters may find it even harder to cope with the daily mechanics of being a student and athlete.

Interdisciplinary Learning

Student-athletes encounter school support staff for a variety of reasons. Support staff deal with their personal, academic, and behavioral issues.

More administrators are awakening to the fact that their guidance counselors, social workers, coaches and psychologists are grossly underutilized in their school buildings. Amidst the career, academic and college counseling, school guidance counselors have little time or willpower to engage youth in a proactive manner. More schools are trying to transform the role of these support educators who aid in the overall psychosocial adaptation of school youth.

Instead of guidance counselors, social workers, deans of students, coaches and psychologists addressing student problems after the fact, they should be involved with the students as an essential part of the daily educational experience. Support educators are able to teach group counseling strategies, conflict resolution, self-discipline, confidentiality, and time management as part of the core curriculum credits or at least as an elective. Guidance counselors, social workers, psychologists, coaches and deans of students are already on the payroll, why not let them teach these principles to students in a proactive fashion in the classroom? In doing so, youth will learn to self-manage much sooner and easier, thus alleviating some of the issues that interfere with their academic and athletic development before those issues become obstacles.

It is said: AN OUNCE OF PREVENTION COSTS LESS THAN A POUND OF CURE...It costs less to stop a problem than to solve one.

Educators can learn a lot from this example because we already know that 90% of the problems students are having with academics and athletics have nothing to do with academics and athletics; but nearly 99% of the time they spend in school does not address those psycho-social issues that impede their academic/athletic prosperity. If school buildings could allow more time for students' self-improvement, it would lead to a significant transformation of the average student and athlete.

Health & Wellness

More than 15% of our schoolchildren are considered overweight (Centers for Disease Control and Prevention [CDC], 2000), reaching at least 95% of the Body-Mass Index-for-age barometer. The variety of food choices available to youth and the lack of sustained physical activity at home and school are the basis for the childhood obesity problem in American youth. Schools and families are the unwilling catalysts to the rise in childhood obesity. The schools' cafeterias and vending machines provide meals to youth who are in the school building for 9-10 months of the year, six to eight hours daily. The schools also provide the physical education programs (or lack of) which help students to burn off excess energy and calories (Van Steveren, 2004).

Many youngsters are running the risk of developing cardiovascular disease, high blood pressure, diabetes and other maladies because of their excessive/deficient food intake and exercise regimen. Obesity has not only a physical toll but a psychological one as well (Schwimmer, Burwinkle, & Varni, 2003), impairing the lives of young men and women who should be able to enjoy all of the activities and opportunities afforded them in school (Van Steveren, 2004).

Some of the contributing factors to the problem of childhood obesity are:

1. Unhealthy Foods in Schools: 1 in 5 schools offer brand-name fast food meals in their schools; many soft drink manufacturers have "pouring rights" agreements with schools and youth athletic programs; junk food vending machines give students access to mounds of "sugar on the go" with a proliferation of pre-packaged snacks

2. Limited Physical Activity in Schools: limited opportunities to engage in age-appropriate physical activity; decreasing budgets cause many schools to abandon athletic and physical education programs (however the cost to treat obesity-related disease may be even higher than providing schools with gym teachers, coaches, equipment, buses and balls);

3. Unhealthy Foods in Family Life: the food industry spends over $30 billion dollars per annum on promotions and advertising to influence parents' food buying decisions; convenient food items that are pre-packaged, canned, microwaveable, pre-heated and frozen help families to feed themselves betwixt their hectic lifestyles and schedules—(Van Steveren, 2004).

By Any Means Necessary—Help Them Further Their Education

The economic reality in this nation is that every youngster needs to further his/her professional training beyond high school. As they expand their knowledge they enhance their opportunities for career success, which positions them to financially provide for their families when they are independent adults. Students gain access to higher education by different means. Some get there by way of the drum (the arts); others by way of the pen (academics); still others by way of their legs (athletics). It is unfair and rather bigoted for adults, especially school officials, to "de-value" the manner in which a student gains access to higher learning. Student- athletes in our society, depending on the prevailing attitudes of their school community, are often discouraged to maximize on the opportunity to go to college by way of athletics; as if it is some kind of "lesser-than" method of college acceptance.

Athletes graduating from high school and entering into college can only help the school student body to realize they can create additional options for themselves in pursuit of advanced degrees. It is critical that students recognize that there are colleges out there that may appreciate their artistic, academic, and/or athletic skills and performance. It is also critical that everyone in the school building understands that access to college via academic, arts or athletics is no *gimme*; it is earned through sweat, toil and sacrifice. Once that ideal is promoted throughout the school community, more people in the school will develop a healthier respect for the persons in pursuit of college access regardless of their preferred routes.

Based on environmental, social and financial factors, students will take different routes to realize a college dream. Not surprisingly, many college-level athletes have "experiences, aptitudes, and socioeconomic backgrounds" that are vastly different from the general student body (Wolniak, et al 2001). The preparation of student-athletes for college rests with the student him/herself, the secondary school faculty, parents and of course, coaches.

Coaching

The job of coaching is HARD. Coaches have to be concerned about their private lives, their public image as well as the health and welfare of their players. If they work inside the school building, they'll have the additional responsibility for the welfare of the entire student body, security of the building, and management of the school facilities. In addition, the asinine policies and procedures of the National Collegiate Athletic Association make it a separate full-time job for high school coaches to help youth to migrate to intercollegiate athletics.

All of this pressure makes it tough for coaches to maintain their sanity and social decorum. Regardless of the pressure, coaches have to be able to keep their cool and avoid harshly criticizing players and officials publicly (Gilbert et al, 2007). Coaches should offer praise when athletes perform to their ability (Smoll & Smith, 2002) even when they are unsuccessful (Gilbert et al, 2007). When athletes make mistakes, coaches should meet them with encouragement and "technical instruction" to uplift and re-direct the athlete (Gilbert et al, 2007). When coaches and players agree to their expectations of each other, there is a greater chance for a cohesive and profitable relationship between them.

Coaches should be required to attend coaching clinics and seminars. Teaching techniques must evolve over time and so does coaching techniques. Coaching is merely teaching on the field. The field is an extension of the classroom. Coaches who don't understand the intricacies of their sport are teaching their players everything they know and consequently handicapping their players; especially in football where a lack of wisdom and training can get a player seriously hurt on the field.

Coaching seems to have lost the respect it had in past years. When a coach spoke, players would listen and respond. Some of it is consistent with a pervasive lack for authority that is more common among youth today.

The tone for every individual player and the entire team has to be set by the Coach. Standards of behavior were set by the coach throughout his/her program in years past. Not so much today. Parents want to tell coaches how to run their teams and manage their children on the field. Kids hear negativity at home and internalize it all the way to the field. No parent has the full insight and knowledge into a coach's athletic program. Therefore, parents are in no position to publicly criticize a coach. Society has plenty of arm-chair quarterbacks and couch potato point-guards who think they know more about the game than the people who teach it every day.

Michael Carrington is a high school football coach in the Prince George's County Maryland area who has sights on trying to prepare his guys for life on and off the field. Part of his challenge, like many other coaches, is to weigh the input and energy parents have in their young athletes against the need for structure and uniformity in any athletic program.

"I think the most challenging obstacle facing high school coaches and athletes is parents with unrealistic goals and expectations for their children. Many of them still see athletics as THE TICKET to a better life for their kids (and themselves) and as such, have unrealistic assessments of their child's athletic ability. This in turn leads to feelings of hostility toward the coach when the coach has an opposite view of their child's playing ability and ambivalence toward the athletic program when the child does not receive what the parent feels is a sufficient opportunity to compete", Carrington weighs in.

Obviously this is taken from a coach's viewpoint but the interesting thing about Carrington is that he, too, has a son playing football in the same program. Carrington says that he made certain that he tried not to prejudice his coaches one way or the other about his son's abilities and potential. He only wishes that more parents across the nation took a similar approach.

Parents and coaches need to figure out a way to work together in the best interest of all of the participants on a team because a failure to do so will ultimately distract coaches from their main objectives. Carrington posits, "The thing I have learned this year as a high school coach, especially coaching a junior varsity-level football team dominated by freshmen, is to have more patience with players who are in the process of adapting to a high school environment. Their attention spans have yet to expand to the necessary level and the process of guiding them to that level can be very exasperating for a coach."

It is human nature for a parent to question a call or dislike a play but it is how it is handled by the parent that either builds up the esteem of a program or tears it down. If a coach's guidance is just so egregiously counterproductive to a child's growth and development, parents should be able to address that with the coach or in rare cases, take their child of the team. Nothing good can be gained by leaving our children on a team to suffer as we run to and fro spewing our internal combustion to whomever we can find…and nearly all of us parents are guilty of it!

There is no question that there are a lot of coaches who poorly teach and train our youth. Fortunately in America, parents have a right to coach, teach and train their own kid instead of leaving it for someone else to do it. But, when a parent decides to allow his child to continue participation in a program, the parent has an obligation to let the child grow up in that program with little or no interference from the parent.

However, coaches can also make it a little easier on parents by giving them a format to express their concerns and feelings. Some coaches give parents an "inside look" at their program in order to build rapport and mutual respect with parents. Others use email and instant messaging to better communicate with parents.

Regardless of the method, if coaches set up a process for parents to express themselves, it should diminish conflict and confrontation between them.

State Of School Athletics

In an anonymous article appearing in the Journal of Physical Education, it is reported that there are nearly equal numbers of sports offered for girls and boys in school settings (Anonymous, 2007).

In a survey of athletic programs, more than three quarters of the schools experienced athletic budget challenges, "primarily related to the lack of support from school district funds" (Anonymous, 2007). In most public schools, "school board funds remained the top source of athletics' budget dollars, accounting for more than 46 percent of the budget. Revenue generated from student activity, sports tickets, and gate receipts make up about 32 percent of the average athletics budget, followed by booster club activities (almost 10%) and supplemental fundraising (about 7%). While many schools have increasingly resorted to athletics' participation fees, "pay-to-play" dollars make up only about 6 percent of the average athletics budget." In private schools, student tuition pays for the athletic programs with a little help from fundraising and game ticket sales" (Anonymous, 2007).

The survey also determined that coach gender barriers are being crossed in high school athletics. "Among boys' teams, females coached more than 25 percent of swimming and diving, 14 percent of volleyball, nearly 14 percent of tennis, and approximately 13 percent of cross-country. Among girls' teams, males coached 14 percent of basketball, roughly 12 percent of track and field and cross-country, and about 11 percent of soccer" (Anonymous, 2007). Women's sports programs have made monumental and triumphant progress over the years thanks in large part to Title IX legislation.

Title IX is a landmark policy that aims at leveling the athletic "playing field" for women on the collegiate level. Title IX was federally mandated in 1971 to give equal educational and athletic access to women in schools that receive federal funds (Lee, 1997). NCAA Division One football and men's basketball are the major breadwinners in most athletic departments and women's sports have historically been commercially underdeveloped in America. To help balance the scales in terms of athletic departments' commitment of resources to women's sports, Title IX was reinforced by school districts nationwide and the NCAA.

The impact of women's participation in sports has had a rippling effect since the turn of the century that has caught even the casual observer's eye. In a New York Times Upfront article, the feats of noted female athletes like 13-year-old Michelle Wie who tied for 47th place in a field of 96 men in a professional golf qualifying event in Hawaii, 17-year-old Kim Salma who became the first girl to win a wrestling match in the New Jersey state finals against boys and place-kicker Katie Hnida who was the first woman to take the field in a men's Division 1-A college football game are highlighted as evidence of their impact (Longman & Zack 2003).

The overall popularity of women' sports and women competing in male-dominated sports are growing in America. The successes of the U.S. women's Olympic soccer, basketball and softball teams, and track and field are etched in the minds and hearts of many Americans and ultimately, Madison Avenue and Wall Street. Despite these developments, some athletic departments are still wishy-washy about their own women's sports programs.

Secondary School Programs

Secondary school athletic programs can be utilized by any school to boost enrollment, scholarship and fundraising. Once a school has a good athletic program (and male and female athletes are going to college via athletics) they start to attract a broader diversity of students; as a result, other programs in the school benefit from it (e.g. Band, Fine Arts, Academic and Outreach programs). School administrations should be 100% behind athletics because it could only improve students' daily way of life and enhance school functions. When administrations are behind their athletic programs, they help to provide the necessary physical, fiscal and philosophical resources to strengthen their sports programs. When they are not fully supportive, it can be a frustrating, daunting and intimidating task for coaches, parents and players to create an environment conducive for excellence in athletic competition.

On the academic side, school faculty personnel should view the athletic playing field as an extension of the classroom. Learning and life skills are not only taught in the classroom but through sports as well. There is some evidence suggesting that participation in "revenue producing" sports (i.e., intercollegiate football and basketball) may engage a peer subculture not present in non-revenue producing sports (Wolniak, et al, 2001). Therefore, it may be more difficult for faculty to penetrate the psyche of football and basketball players and coaches. By interweaving the distinct domains of athletics and academics, student-athletes have a much better chance of excelling in class as well; assuming that is everyone's goal. The classroom offers a prime opportunity for faculty members to integrate the lessons learned from the playing field to the lessons taught in their class. However, there are occasions when there is mutual lack of respect between educators and coaches and it can lead to disharmony in the school community and disorient the student-athletes.

If the faculty and coaches can work together (easier said than done), they will discover that the school will produce more well-rounded student-athletes; athletes who understand that academics and athletics are of similar dimension. A student that is organized and studies hard is the athlete that is coachable, works hard and is less prone to error. Faculty and coaches working together can help build men and women of strong values and character.

On every campus, there are students, athletes and coaches who believe that student athletes' academic participation takes a backseat to their roles as athletes. In fact, many student athletes are very committed to their academic progress and have a tremendous respect for faculty members who try to cultivate good working relationships with them (Harrison et al, 2006). Yet many college-level athletes do not complete their degrees as quickly as non-athlete students and earn lower grades (Dudley et al, 1997). But many of the revenue-producing athletes (basketball/football) maintained similar curricula standards and graduation rates as the general student body (Wolniak, et al, 2001).

Health & Sports

It is tragic to see many school districts struggle to finance physical education programs in their schools. For many youth, the exercise they get during P.E. class is the only supervised exercise they get at all. Everyone is not going to be a competitive athlete and intramural athletic activities and gym classes provide a rich alternative to the youngsters. As the nation confronts the obesity of its youth, supervised athletic participation should be in vogue.

Children need to be active in sports and physical recreation but the reduction in intramural and P.E. opportunities due to declining budgets is making it more difficult for schools to get them the exercise they need. (Stewart et al, 2005).

In the absence of the supervised athletic games, youngsters turn more to virtual, simulated and unsupervised play games. Consequently, that can lead to an even more sedentary physical and mental lifestyle (Stewart et al, 2005).

The Value of Sport in Society

Relationships

The relationships that are developed during athletic competition can be very special and unique; especially in team sports. Relationships between players and coaches, players and players, and coaches and coaches can be bonded by the countless hours they spend together studying, training, and competing.

Those relationships will extend beyond the playing field and throughout a lifetime. Those teammates can be called upon during tough times even after the playing days are over. After the athletic career ends, most players cannot recall most of the games but they do remember the interaction and kinships between battle mates. As those teammates become members of an extended family, those relationships provide comfort and confidence to players forever. One such story involves former

Dallas Cowboys' teammates Ron Springs and Everson Walls. Springs needed a kidney transplant and Walls was the donor nearly a decade and a half after they retired from football.

Then there is the relationship with the sport itself. When you are involved in an activity for most of your life, in a way, it defines who and what you are. A piece of it stays with you for the rest of your life. When the games come to an end, you lose a part of your identity. It is human nature to experience anxieties and depression associated with that loss. For many, they have been riding on a high from the competition for most of their lives and suddenly the down side of that high is traumatic. It is difficult for competitive athletes to face the reality that their careers are over.

A community also creates a relationship with sports programs. Many community members inside of a school or within a neighborhood identify with the players and teams closest to them. Many of the youngsters who play for the local high school were raised in those neighborhoods and adults who watched them grow up will continue to cheer them during their playing days.

There is also a psychological relationship that develops with sports. Sports can have a life-altering effect on anyone involved. How *impactful* can a sports program be? In Syracuse New York, Bubba Grimes had the pleasure (and pain) of overseeing and assisting a few semi-pro football teams. At the time, the City of Syracuse had the highest per capita murder rate and growing concerns with gang violence, street-level drug trafficking, and sporadic violence in the schools. The judicial and legislative Syracuse community highlighted the fact that there was a sharp increase in the violence and criminal mischief of young men between the ages of 19-24. Not so incidentally, that is the post-high school, pre-marriage age for young men. It is the time period when institutional sports comes to a screeching halt unless they are competing for a college or professional team. Perhaps 40% of the semi-pro players in Grimes' programs had some kind of adult criminal record associated with drugs or violence before they joined the teams.

Yet during those football campaigns, of the over 100 players involved with those teams in Central New York, scarcely 2% of them had any legal run-ins.

Grimes and his compatriots noticed that these young men on the semi-pro circuit were going home at night to rest their bodies and keeping their day jobs. They were more focused on taking care of their bodies with good nutrition as their smoking and alcohol consumption dropped. Not one player entered a drug rehab facility or a correctional facility during those football seasons. They brought their wives, girlfriends and children (even those who were estranged) to their football games.

When the seasons' ended, one in twenty of these young men would commit crimes that landed them in prison compared to the one in fifty during the season.

Grimes, former Orangeman Jerome Hall, and long-time friend Duane Milton petitioned the school systems, elected officials, and community groups who were complaining and writhing over the "lost generation" of males to provide some financial support to keep the programs viable. They discovered that it was a very cost-effective way to battle crime in the area. Statistics revealed that it costs nearly $39,000 per year to keep a young man locked behind bars. Through the semi-pro network, it would cost $5,000 per man to keep them involved in the football programs year-round. They asked these civic and municipal groups to provide some consistent and significant funding for these amateur adult football programs so more young men could have an alternative to a life of crime.

Nary would an agency, politician or institution answer the call.

Reciprocal Benefit

"Give, and it shall be given unto you; good measure, pressed down and shaken together, and running over, shall men give into your bosom. For with the same measure that ye mete withal it shall be measured to you again"

Luke 6:38 KJV

Many student-athletes are accustomed to giving back to their communities. Athletic teams are frequently called upon to help other community members with community projects, etc. Athletic teams are perhaps the easiest group of students to assemble because they usually travel together and are aware of each others' strengths and weaknesses. They know who speaks well in public and who is too nervous. They know who has physical stamina and who doesn't. They know who values fashion and who couldn't care less about style. Therefore, whenever an athletic team is called upon to help with something in their neighborhood or school community, they generally manage projects quickly and efficiently.

For the few athletes who make it to a Division One college and/or professional-paid level, they are renowned for giving money, support, and status to many charitable events. Everyone that makes it to the NFL or the NBA specifically gives money back to their communities and charities. They also give their time! Many of them sponsor free camps and family seminars. Athletes like NBA's Dikembe Mutombo fight for humanitarian causes in their native countries. Many of them lend their status to causes related to academic achievement, substance abuse, and fights for the cure of cancer and HIV-AIDS. Unfortunately, much of it is drowned out today in the media by the occasional spectacle of an OJ Simpson saga or Alex Rodriguez drama.

Adversity Training

"GOD is our refuge and strength, a very present help in trouble. Therefore will not we fear, though the earth be removed, and though the mountains be carried into the midst of the sea; Though the waters thereof roar and be troubled, though the mountains shake with the swelling thereof"

Psalm 46:1-3 KJV

For parents, educators and students, adversity is an integral part of the maturation process. No matter how well we raise our children, they are going to get into stuff and stuff is going to get into them. Just because we experience adversity does not mean that we've done something wrong to deserve it. The Bible tells us that GOD's rain falls on the just and unjust alike. It is important for us to prepare our children for success but at the same time, train them through adversity. Parents and educators could practice adversity "drills"; in football we call it "sudden change." One minute we have the football at the five yard line going in for a touchdown and the next play our opponent runs our fumble back to our five yard line. The teams who practice "sudden change" are better equipped to handle its onset.

The best part of athletics is the adversity that is built into every game and practice. There are times when things go the way they were planned and other times everything seems to go completely wrong and you have to deal with it. We should teach youth to embrace adversity, and deal with it head on because life requires that of them when they become adults.

Team sports and activities have a built-in accountability structure that forces participants to overcome adversity for the good of the team. The short term affect is that team activities depend on each participant to hold up their end of the deal; or at least try like heck. When someone doesn't, team peers may look upon them as "quitters" who didn't keep his/her commitment. Coaches preach to youth that success is a habit and failure is too. If a person develops a pattern of quitting when things get tough on the playing field, he/she may continue to do the same thing throughout life.

Things will rarely go the way a student-athlete plans. There are going to be humps that they have to work to get over. Sometimes a student-athlete has no control over the situation but always has control over the response. Here's an example of each:

One student-athlete was forced by his coach in college to move from his preferred position to a position that he had not played since high school. When he was told of the move he wanted to leave school for another school. His father would not let him switch schools. As an adult today, when he is faced with adversity, he always tries to find the positive lesson in it and work through the challenge.

There was another student-athlete in the same situation. He was always enabled by his parents who habitually made excuses for him when he did not perform well at anything. Although the coaches told him what they expected of him to excel at the new position, he never accepted the challenge and did not make an effort to improve. When faced with the same situation in college, he quit the team.

Perhaps the greatest lesson in life a young person can learn is:

BRYCE K. BEVILL

No One in this Life gets a Free Ride...We have to pay for Who we are and What we want

School and athletics are the greatest gifts our youth can have in this American civilization today. They offer every opportunity for youth to practice and prepare for life's eventual challenges. When a young person proactively deals with adversity at school or on the playing field, he/she is preparing for life. For the youth who want to prepare for life and overcome adversity along the way, here are a few tips:

-don't skip practice
-don't skip homework
-condition yourself to bring your "A" game everyday
-don't look for the easy way out
-everyone is not going to like you
-you will show others respect and treat them kindly and some of them will still punch you in the mouth for no apparent reason; and so will life itself

ESPN began running a series during the 2007 college football season called Lou Holtz's Pep Talk. Holtz is a highly sought-after motivational speaker and it is obvious why he is so coveted. In a pep talk to Michigan after their embarrassing loss to Appalachian State in the season opener that year, Holtz offered a pep talk to the Wolverines to help them focus in on their next opponent. In this talk he reminded them that in life, "a pink slip will be on your office desk, the car will get repossessed, and you'll come home and your four kids will tell you that Mommy has run off with the drummer. Now what are you going to do?" (or something to that effect).

Holtz suggested to the Wolverines to store up all of their negative energy and release it on their next opponent. In other words, he said that someone would have to pay for what happened to them the week before and it might as well be the team they're playing Saturday. He was trying to help them to turn a negative/adverse situation into a progressive, positive outcome at the earliest possible opportunity. They would have to work hard to get there but the work itself would be part of the recovery.

"A merry heart doeth good like a medicine: but a broken spirit drieth the bones"

Proverbs 17:22

When things don't go well, youngsters must be careful not to dwell on their misfortune too long or stare too long at the success of others. This will help them avoid feeling sorry for themselves or growing envious of others.

Feelings of self-pity can beset anyone but no one can afford to wallow in it.

CHAPTER THREE
FAITH & DISCIPLINE

"Now faith is the substance of things hoped for, the evidence of things not seen"

Hebrews 11:1 KJV

Spirituality is based on a belief in GOD and attendance at traditional, regular worship services (DiIulio, 2002). Spiritual development is known for defeating the human passion to hustle, steal, kill, get high and do dirt to our brother. One such story of a man named Jeffrey Hood eclipses the notion that tigers can never change their stripes. A self-proclaimed junior gangster, Hood spent many days and nights selling marijuana and crack cocaine. His path is a model of how beautiful, healthy and vibrant young boys somehow engage in decrepit, debilitating, self-effacing social behavior (Stodghill, 2005).

Upon entering high school, Hood fell into a group of peers who engaged in anti-social gang-related antics. He first broke into a school to steal computers and then escalated to selling dope after spending a year in a juvenile detention center. Like many youth, Hood's penchant for pursuing the wrong was not diminished by his correctional detainment; just the opposite, jail fueled it. His interest in smoking weed, making money from his hustle, and chasing the honeys led to poor academic performance and eventually dropping out of school. It is the same story for hundreds of thousands of young men in America over the past two decades (Stodghill, 2005).

"Let him that stole steal no more. But rather let him labor, working with his hands the thing which is good, that he may have to give to him that needeth"

Ephesians 4:28 KJV

Hood's path changed direction when he landed a legit job for a boss who helped him navigate his course and took him to church. His boss, Mr. Harris was willing to give Hood a chance to earn an honest living when most employers are reluctant to hire ex-convicts. Many times, the desire to give wanna-be thugs a second chance does not amount to much more than an employers' sleepless nights and stolen inventory. A Princeton University study revealed that employers are reluctant to hire people with drug-related offenses, especially African-Americans. However, when a spiritual component is reinforced, youngsters have a much better chance to walk away from the dirty and pursue the narrow road to achievement. In the end, by walking the straight and narrow way, the Hoods of the world can still have money in their pockets and meet worthy female companions; which in most cases were their reasons for doing criminal things in the first place (Stodghill, 2005).

"Therefore if any man be in Christ, he is a new creature. Old things are passed away; behold, all things are become new"
                                                    2 Corinthians 5:17 KJV

Faith In Action

Youth must be steadfast in their goals if they want to build positive character and pursue academic and athletic excellence. Youth are learning valuable lessons everyday at home, school and on the playground to build their resolve for life's challenges. All of them will be tested time and again throughout their journey. One of the keys to weathering storms as they come is for youth to develop and practice faith. Those youth who build and practice a strong faith ethic are better equipped for life's ups and downs than those who don't build their faith foundation.

Children develop faith that is deeply rooted in attitudes and feelings from an early age. Then it matriculates into a unique and significant relationship with their deity as they get older and become responsible and accountable to their faith practices (Chromey 2006). Faith is best nurtured in the home as ground zero as older children grow to reflect their parents/grandparents' faith practices (Chromey, 2006). Faith has life-transforming qualities that transcend barriers that seem insurmountable (DiIulio 2002). Faith in action can improve youth's self-esteem and self-acceptance especially when they are feeling insecure about themselves.

Regardless of what anyone says negatively about them, they can see their own wondrous beauty and uniqueness as creations of GOD. The images seen on television and in magazines set trends and standards for too many youth. The desire or desperation to "fit-in" can cause a youth to feel that he/she is substandard in some ways, leading to anxiety and depression. By looking in the mirror or into one's own soul in the context of being GOD's creation, a youngster is able to shed those feelings of inferiority and celebrate his/her individual characteristics. Like snowflakes, every person has his/her individual attributes made in the likeness of GOD. Therefore, GOD could be both tall and short, round and thin, black and white, big lipped and thin lipped, temperamental and cool, shy and outgoing, and any other characteristic we find in ourselves and others (Heiberg, 2006).

Viewing oneself in the context of being GOD's unique creation will also empower youth to change things about themselves that can be changed. Whether it's a hairstyle change, gaining or losing weight, or making slight wardrobe adjustments, youth can execute these changes easier when they take their eyes off of media images and close their ears to their peers and focus on GOD's greatness in them (Heiberg, 2006).

Faith development is not an isolated or snappy process. It is not a sprint but a marathon that lasts a lifetime; albeit a marathon through high mountains and deep valleys. Faith is also built in a tailor-made fashion, taking into account individual personalities, interests, and upbringings (Chromey 2006).

Young children initially make faith commitments based on following someone such as a teacher, pastor, Jesus or friend. Their faith marinates in a "family-centered" arena with a community of believers with like faith commitments. As the community of members shift with time, youth solidify their faith commitment with a belief in something that will always remain a constant. In the Christian faith, Jesus is a symbol or entity which is omnipresent and omnipotent. Jesus can be enjoyed for longer than a season and in the presence of other community members on the mountaintops and in the valley lows (Chromey 2006).

Character develops as faith progresses because moral behavior is based less on reward & punishment and more on personal accountability for people with growing faith. Teachers, coaches and parents play an all-important role as they affirm positive moral character by acknowledging it to their youth instead of giving them inducements to behave such as gifts and prizes (Chromey, 2006).

Older children are able to crystallize the world inside and around them better than when they were younger. Their ability to form abstract thought transcends the boundaries of space and time. They begin to think critically and hypothetically and it is perhaps the most significant transformation for humans. At this juncture, abstract rituals and ceremonies such as communion and baptism are more meaningful and purposeful. Older children begin to associate these rituals with broader, deeper aspects of their faith such as sin and salvation (Chromey, 2006).

Many youth also make moral decisions based more on peer influence than their own personal convictions. Quite a few of them have to isolate or compartmentalize themselves from some of their peers in order to feel comfortable with their moral choices. Some are coaxed by peers to choose the wrong path whether it's by cheating on exams or sneaking a co-ed under the bleachers. The pull can be very strong, especially when it seems like all of the other kids are doing it. Again, this is where the relationship with their "higher power" plays a pivotal role because that authority will give them the strength to buck their peers' influence (Chromey, 2006).

As children become more peer-conscious, they are attuned to their strengths and weakness as they become more self-reliant. Sports are one of the activities which daily reveal some of their assets and weaknesses and offer opportunities to improve upon them. Children eventually choose which sports they prefer to participate in based on the value they feel they get from them. It is through these chosen experiences that youth are able to build their faith foundations in real-world, real-time venues. Children find similar venues with their hobbies and interests including the arts, academic disciplines, and social relationships (Chromey, 2006).

Parent/Child/Community Faith

There is perhaps a universal need to have more youth/adult interactive communities where they learn in conjunction with each other. One form of faith development is a spirituality which develops from or expressed in individual participation in outreach programs run by institutions with a religious slant (DiIulio, 2002). These can happen in academic, religious and athletic settings. By engaging youth in projects and activities which require an exchange of ideals between child/parent, student/teacher, and coach/player, youth and adults can gain insight into each others psyche. In the Christian faith this means to assist them in their daily walk with Christ (Chromey, 2006).

There is a sense of youth being more spiritual today than ever but it is grounded in "believing" more than "belonging." Institutional religion may be less of a force in their lives than the interest in serving the needs of others in their community (Kaufman, 2003).

Faith is a very active practice in today's society with spiritually-based online chat groups, and more faith-based civic outreach projects, supported by government, that deal with academic skills and social ills (Kaufman, 2003).

Public-private partnerships between government and faith-based programs play "significant roles in community development, welfare-to-work programs, day care, and other areas." In the U.S. Conference of Mayors (2001), the city leaders overwhelmingly supported a furtherance of such relationships and expanding its network with local community ministries (DiIulio 2002). According to Robert Woodson of the National Center for Neighborhood Enterprise, these types of collaborative programs instill a sense of trust among participants which may account for some of its effectiveness (DiIulio 2002).

It is difficult to use public funds to support religious movements or promote a particular religious belief in schools. But municipal bodies are allowed to contract with faith-based organizations to deliver outreach programs, including literacy enhancement, substance abuse interdiction, and welfare to work (DiIulio, 2002). As well, too many youth are living in environments where adults are absent. Subsequently, they are forced to create their own value systems and social order (Kaufman, 2003). Community-based collaborations can help youth to define their value systems and function within society's prescribed norms.

Other national faith-based programs like the Prison Fellowship Ministries sponsor drug-treatment and educational support to incarcerated persons. Current data suggest that these types of organizations have had a sustained positive impact on the well-being and improvement of the people it serves. Led by former Watergate convict Charles Colson, this program boasts a much smaller recidivism rate for inmates in the program than those who are not (DiIulio, 2002).

Another program, Philadelphia's Youth Education for Tomorrow (YET), offers an after-school program in conjunction with other churches, schools and programs in the area. Youth in the YET program showed a significant increase in their reading level. Those results are typical of such organizations which collaborate with non-religious organizations, civic clubs, and educational institutions (DiIulio 2002). Under President Bush, the Ready4Work program allocated $300 million for faith-based programs. These initiatives are geared to help participants secure employment and provide support such as mentoring and prison-to-work. Coupled with a religious influence, these types of outreach services help counteract negative social influences (DiIulio 2002).

Youth are more inclined to overcome the negative effects of violence, poverty, peer pressure, etc. when they have a consistent relationship with a religious organization (DiIulio, 2002). Folks who believe in GOD and attend regularly scheduled worship services are believed to experience less drug/alcohol abuse, depression and hyper-sensitivity than those who don't have a formal faith in GOD. Youth who worship are believed to have more control over sexual desires, succeed academically, and exhibit more positive character traits than youth who don't go to worship services (DiIulio, 2002).

"But without faith it is impossible to please him, for he that cometh to GOD must believe that he is, and that he is a rewarder of them that diligently seek him"

Hebrews 11:6 KJV

Religion & School

To compensate for the challenges facing youth today with the disintegrating family, neighborhoods, and public schools, some parents turn to private schools where religion is openly taught and spiritual worship is a norm. As much as people advocate for spirituality as a means to combat social ills, there is an aggressive push to keep religion out of our nation's public schools. Beyond an occasional "moment of silence" school leaders are petrified of civil lawsuits whenever they promote Christian faith and deviate from established school curricula (Gheezi, 2007).

Private-religious schools can cost a pretty penny, ranging $7,000 to $25,000 per year. Parents who send their children to private schools are not exempt from paying school taxes to support public schools; in effect paying twice for one education (Gheezi, 2007). Many of these private schools not only teach religious doctrine but teach state-mandated math, science and english as well (Gheezi, 2007) and should be reimbursed by the states because they reduce the potential for even more crowded public school classrooms. However, two recent court decisions may have an impact on spiritual outreach to youth in public schools:

Case #1-

A South Dakota teacher won a lawsuit against school officials who objected to her participation in a Christian after-school program that meets at the school. The district did not want to give the impression that they are promoting Christianity in their schools (Anonymous, 2003).

Case #2-

An Arizona court determined that a school district must disseminate literature about an after-school program that has an underlying religious agenda (Anonymous, 2003).

Christianity is widely believed to be available to anyone who wants to engage it, but just not in public school. In the faith, Christ is characterized as the vine, the cornerstone, and the truth and the life (Johnson-Siebold, 2005). Without the vine, the branches wither and decease. Since children spend the bulk of their waking hours at school, many people want them to continue to get a consistent dose of Christ there. The argument for Christian inclusion, the separation of church and state withstanding, is that Christ does not exist separate from the rest of society and should be integrated wherever children desire. Human beings' desperate calls for justice, equality, and hospitality are espoused in true Christian service, as the example of Jesus' life teaches (Johnson-Siebold, 2005). These desperate calls are heard nowhere as loudly than in the halls of our nation's public academies.

Power of Prayer

Prayer and meditation is a common practice among people with faith aspirations. Prayer is even identified as an important process in seeking improved health. A Johns Hopkins' medical study discovered 9 in 10 adults in their care believed in GOD and 80% of them wanted their physicians to include spirituality in their treatment (Kogan, 2006). Individual and group prayer is used to strengthen the morale and spirit of sick persons. Prayer is used as an "intercession" when one prays on behalf of another ill person (Kogan, 2006).

Physicians aware of their patients' spiritual beliefs will incorporate aspects of it into their primary care. One of the biggest changes in health care itself is the increase in medical schools that are offering courses in spirituality. Among the 70 medical schools incorporating the spiritual model, they are gathering faith history information as well as medical and family history info on their patients (Kogan, 2006).

Further studies show that spiritual worship positively affects the immune system and enhances the endorphins in the brain. This is very good news for people who experience chronic illness or "non-specific" maladies.

Since doctors can't see and hear spirituality, it is hard for them to quantify its medical value (Kogan, 2006). Visible to the naked eye or not, there is evidence to support spirituality as a means of improving mental and physical health as well as balancing some of our social problems (DiIulio, 2002).

The Art of Self-Mastery

It's January, again. Just like last January we are committed to losing or managing the weight. The doctors have told us that we need to lose a few pounds or a lot of pounds. Our knees and ankles are asking us for mercy. Every time we shop for clothes, we...we...oh just forget about shopping for clothes. We'll do that after we lose a few more pounds.

The holidays are over and we figured we made the last excuse. We bought that workout gear and exercise machine as a Christmas present to ourselves. Some of us even paid the down payment and contracted for two years at the gym. We bought that Bob Greene diet and life-changing book we saw on Oprah. We testified in church and witnessed to our loved ones that this is the year for change.

We start out like a house on fire as we watch "The Biggest Loser" every Tuesday night for inspiration. Funny thing is, they are losing weight every show, and we are not.

Then the luncheons start up at work. Our team lost in the playoffs and we're bummed out so we eat to comfort our wounds. Suddenly, the blast of cold, frigid arctic air arrives and we'll be darned if we are going back out in that stuff, gym or no gym.

Soon, we are sampling just a taste of the forbidden fruits we said we weren't going to eat this year. Then we sample it again. Late one night, we're having a little trouble resting because that sweet-tasting, mouth-watering, seductive son-of-a-gun is calling our name from the refrigerator. And we've taken care of our needy kids and loved our ungrateful spouse and served our nuisance boss all week and deserve to treat ourselves.

Within no time the sample becomes a compulsion which grows into an addiction and the excuse becomes a rationale and the gym is uncomfortable and our weight rises again.

But all is not lost. Next January is only 6 months away.

Self-Discipline

True self-discipline embodies steady progress toward chosen goals. Self-discipline means self-sacrifice and obedience to time & task required by one's own self or someone in authority over us.

Educators instill self-discipline in youth in a variety of creative ways. As an example, a karate studio teaches values to their students by having them pay for their lessons through service to the community. Instructors believe martial arts teach self-control and respect. In many instances, youth learn how to focus better which helps them in school (Wagner, 2007). In helping youth to build their self-confidence and self-worth, martial arts is a way to teach youth self-defense techniques and the volunteer aspect helps them to think less about themselves and more about the needs of others (Keyser, 2007). Plus, karate programs are good ways to help youth to manage their weight, increase strength and of course, achieve discipline (Wagner, 2007).

Self-discipline techniques can be developed by anyone, old or young, male or female. There is some debate about whether boys are by nature less able to exhibit self-control than girls (Davis, 2007). Girls are reported to achieve better grades than boys in secondary school. In a study of students in Philadelphia (Journal of Educational Psychology, February 2006) the girls apparently studied each night twice as much as the boys (Davis, 2007).

Even in the midst of pursuing a worthwhile goal, we all stumble. Sometimes the stumble is accidental and other times it is on purpose (self-sabotage). Self-sabotage is the practice of knowing what to do to achieve goals, yet doing the opposite. Especially when it comes to diet and exercise, choices are habitually made which defy healthy outcomes. The poor choices are made over and again until one day obesity, diabetes, or heart problems result (Kat, 2006). Addictions develop just that way: Occasional or recreational consumption becomes a growing need which intensifies with each trip until it becomes an out-of-control compulsion (Kat, 2006).

By consistently using self-discipline techniques, the urge to fall off the wagon goes down quite a bit.

Self-Management

Self-management incorporates self-monitoring which is the ability to examine and document one's own behavior. Self-management also involves self-assessment which means the ability to identify strengths and weaknesses. Self-instruction is also included in a self-management process that uses self-talk and positive words and phrases to guide our steps. Research speaks to the value of self-management attributes in improving student classroom behavior, especially among those with emotional/behavioral disorders (Callicott & Park, 2003). Close cousins to self-management are self-direction, self-respect, self-perception and self-regulation.

Self-direction is an achievable goal for students with emotional and behavioral problems. These students are two-thirds likely to fail state exams and are less likely to continue their education in college or trade school (Callicott & Park, 2003). Without self-direction strategies, twenty-percent of students with emotional/behavioral disorders get arrested while in school and more than half after they've been out of school a few years (Callicott & Park, 2003).

Self-respect is linked to activities and behaviors. Depending upon dress, attendance, punctuality, behavior, and choices, a student is seen as respecting him/herself or not (Raby, 2005).

Self-perception is the best predictor of a person's capacity to achieve. How one sees him/herself in any situation is a stronger predictor of someone's capacity to achieve than prior success or positive reinforcement (Zinsser, et al, 2004).

Educators/parents should encourage students to exercise control over their own learning and rely less on teachers' and parents' support (Contemporary Women's Issues, 2004). Academic performance is connected to how well learners self-regulate (Contemporary Women's Issues, 2004). For self-regulated learners, their behavior, environment and person are interwoven to advance their learning. Self-regulated learning traits (Contemporary Women's Issues, 2004) allow youth to educate themselves with little prompting by parents or teachers. They become proactive learners and academics become part of a daily discipline.

Students will be internally motivated to perform in school at a lower or higher level and sometimes the pushing and prodding of parents does little to affect that performance. One of the most important things for parents to do is help their children discover reasons to invest time and energy in their academics (Kuhn, 2007). If there is just one objective that motivates a student from within him/herself it may be more than enough. It is not a cookie-cutter approach and will vary from child-to-child (even among siblings) but when the children make the connection between excelling in school and something else that is important to them there is a greater chance for them to be able to push themselves from within. Their internal motivation helps them to identify and address academic problems themselves instead of waiting for someone else to prompt them (Kuhn, 2007).

Sidebar: Lessons from a Martial Arts Instructor—Mixed Martial Arts & Health

Martial arts is a form of activity that not only pushes one to physical, but mental limits. The intricacies of the sport of mixed martial arts or MMA, which has become more popularized in recent years, offers the greater challenge of having a basis in multiple disciplines, thus demanding a greater commitment to careful study. Mixed martial arts draws from ancient fighting art forms from around the world. At its highest form, mixed martial arts are a holistic endeavor that taps the mind—body connection. On the surface, MMA can appear untamed and barbaric, but students of the art understand the intense amount of control and concentration required in its practice. MMA is less about fighting and aggression, and more about the exchange of moves and positions. I would liken it more to human *chess*, than fighting.

Mixed martial arts is valuable in that it teaches one more about themselves than about fighting. This art is for the competitive as well for the hobbyist. It allows one to push themselves to the limits that they desire. Any disciplined instructor and academy will allow one to determine their course individually. MMA helps to instill confidence and a sense of accomplishment, particularly in the youth. Friendships and lasting bonds are created among children that study this unique art together. MMA allows kids to compete individually, yet still remain part of a team or family.

In terms of the health benefits of MMA, it produces results like no other form of physical activity. MMA challenges every muscle in your body, while improving your cardiovascular conditioning. The superior conditioning, strength, and flexibility benefits of MMA have encouraged athletes from other sports to train in the art. Many of the movements and conditioning routines translate directly to other competitive activities. By coupling MMA training with proper diet and nutrition, one is capable of achieving optimum health inside and out. MMA is a great stress reliever and offers a fun alternative to other forms of exercise.

By D'Angelo Kinard, CPT
Thai-Jitsu Practitioner

When Students Ask, "Why Are We Doing This?"

Students are in school to prepare for life and school is what they do to get into college if that is their goal. When youth get into the real world they operate in a world that is vastly different from the one they grew up in. In the real world, everything is done for a purpose and primarily for money. The purposeful nature of adult life is fairly absent in youth and it makes the transition to the real world difficult for anyone (Kuhn, 2007). By helping students early to develop a sense of purpose for their school experience, it will make the adjustment to college and beyond a little easier

When educators focus learning on intellectual "tools" instead of subject matter only, students can better connect their schooling to real life activities (Kuhn, 2007). The intellectual tools such as critical thinking, analytical thinking, inquiry and debate (Kuhn, 2007) make students more versatile and capable of learning different things and adapting to changing environments. Intellectual tools enhance intellectual development which in turn leads to intellectual ownership. Intellectual development occurs at every stage of a child's development but is perhaps ignored by parents and educators the most during middle school years. Intellectual ownership leads to the self-regulation necessary for students to become active learners with energy to pursue their own paths (Kuhn, 2007).

The Parents Again

"A wise son heareth his father's instruction; but a scorner heareth not rebuke"

Proverbs 13:1

Parenting style is a premier factor in children's education (Contemporary Women's Issues, 2004). Correction or discipline is a major parental responsibility. Child-rearing practices vary across economic, cultural and ethnic lines. The cultural values and child-rearing practices preferred by parents sometimes clash with the legal definition of child abuse or neglect (Campbell, 2005). Case in point: Statistically there is a higher percentage of child abuse reported among certain minority children, especially among Native Americans and African Americans. But the interpretation of neglect or abuse is very inconsistent (Campbell, 2005). For example, some public school teachers are allowed to physically discipline their students, providing they have written permission from the parent(s) (Campbell, 2005). In many states, both the teacher and parent would be charged with abuse.

The conflicts between parents and the courts arise when certain parent groups have a belief system that is contrary to the law. There are also cultural child-rearing differences between socioeconomic classes. Studies show that middle class parents allow for a more permissive and authoritative child-rearing style (Campbell, 2005). A "permissive" parenting style prefers to set ground rules for children and include kids in decision-making (Campbell, 2005). "Authoritative" parenting considers the child's viewpoint and upholds the rules of general society. "Authoritarian" style, the preferred method of lower-income households, exercises parental power and includes spanking and other forms of physical correction. Summarily, there are no universal standards and therefore what is considered abuse and neglect in one cultural domain may be an acceptable and expected practice in another (Campbell, 2005).

Mr. Gilbert Hoffman, certified mortgage consultant and investment advisor discusses child-rearing and discipline in the following terms:

"I have always believed that in disciplining our children, we must first hear them out. I often bear witness to parents not giving their children the courtesy of listening first. I feel that it sends the signal that even though a probable punishment is on the horizon, you care about what your child has to say. That being said, I still believe in making the punishment fit the offense. In a world of extreme lifestyles, adding fuel to the fire is not a healthy or effective approach. My parents did not go overboard when my punishment did not require going overboard. They did not let us get away with much, but they used more psychological approaches than physical. I can count the number of times my dad pulled out the belt and heated my behind with it. He and my mom had a way of making me feel so bad about what I did that they did not have to beat the sense into me, most of the time."

"Currently I am raising an 8 year old. She tests the limits of my patience occasionally. I will swat her bottom, but usually it requires implementing a punishment and always explaining why. Additionally, I always ask her why she did what she did. When the crime is severe, the punishment should be too. I must admit that the whole thing is a

work in progress. As she gets older and more mature I do less spanking and more talking. I'll keep you posted on any developments!"

"Pray for me."

Peak Performance

Performance enhancement, similar to those used by military and athletics helps youth to build the right perspective toward success and teaches youth how to use their brains to pursue desired results (Zinsser, et al, 2004). Performance enhancement makes the mind a critical part of the training regimen. In the military, a West Point based training program teaches sports psychology skills such as goal setting, mind control, and stress management with ordinary academic aspects such as exam preparation and note taking. Goal setting is the initial step that helps soldiers and athletes to make acceptable progress in their chosen path (Zinsser, et al, 2004). Goals help people to focus their attention and effort on the task at hand and help achievers to sustain their effort and turn it up when necessary. All youth should set performance goals in academics and athletics.

The results of performance enhancement training will 1) create proper thinking and build self-confidence, 2) improve focus and mental application, 3) teach them to control physiological response to pressures, and 4) maintain a single-minded purpose in pursuit of goals (Zinsser, et al, 2004). The training is designed to enhance performance in academic and leadership through five key components:

A. Understanding how the mind works in pursuit of high performance; gaining confidence and self-control by monitoring self-talk, reprogramming thoughts and beliefs, and developing a powerful self-concept (Zinsser, et al, 2004).

B. Identifying reasons for long-term pursuit of goals and creating an action plan to execute those goals.

C. Paying attention to important external and internal cues to make adjustments along the way. Changing perspectives and expanding awareness; operating in a routine way to make repeat tasks seem simple; pinpoint focus and concentration (keeps one from wasting resources and energies).

D. Recognizing types of stressors and learning to recover and manage energy to avoid burning out.

E. Visualizing desired results and taking steps to attain them; strengthening the will and capacity to move. (Zinsser, et al, 2004).

Getting There

Leaders in both military and athletics try to break their team members down so they can be rebuilt up to the leaders' standards. Many of today's student-athletes who've grown up with permissive and authoritative parenting styles go into shock at their first training session or team practice. The positive net effect of "training camps" is the athlete and soldier learns to depend on each other and learn to trust their leaders. This trusting mindset (Zinsser, et al, 2004) is what is needed for youth to finish each journey. They learn to trust their own abilities, trust the people around them, and trust their leaders so they can freely perform while their opponents are standing there in deep thought not knowing what to do.

Firepower vs. Willpower

"And Jesus answering saith unto them, Have faith in GOD. For verily I say unto you, That whosoever shall say unto this mountain, Be thou removed, and be thou cast into the sea; and shall not doubt in his heart, but shall believe that those things which he saith shall come to pass; he shall have whatsoever he saith"

Mark 11:22-23 KJV

Many students are reluctant to attend certain schools because they fear they will not be able to keep up. Some athletes do not try out for a team for fear they will not stand up to the challenge. Although academic or athletic challenges may seem daunting, the fear of them is proportional to the trust and confidence a student a) has in him/herself, b) those around them, and c) the people teaching them.

When faced with any foe, their advantage over an opponent is strongly determined by the dominion the student has over him/herself. Regardless of the size, speed, and strength of an athletic opponent, a student can still compete with or defeat the opposition. A student's willpower is more of a determining factor in his/her academic and athletic success than the strength of the obstacles in front of them.

Spike Lee and Jim Brown talked about firepower versus willpower in a college lecture program (Syracuse University, 2003). Brown was very concerned at the time about the Bush Administration's desire to invade Iraq. He illustrated the fact that people's willpower cannot be broken by missiles, cannons and mortar; actually, their willpower may even strengthen.

He warned that America was headed on a dangerous course because the people in and around Iraq were not likely to give in no matter how many bombs were dropped on them.

In the movie, "Million Dollar Baby", acting fighter Hilary Swank complained to her trainer about losing to her opponent in the ring. Her trainer, played by Clint Eastwood, promptly explained that her opponent was faster, younger and better and asked her what she was going to do. In essence, her opponent had more firepower. In the next scene, Swank knocked her out cold.

These are a few creative illustrations of how willpower has more power than firepower. Surely firepower makes a difference in any struggle but firepower is limited, can be exhausted, lost, or malfunction. Willpower comes from within and is only limited by the goals and purposes of the individual. If it's important enough, the individual will more often than not find a way to achieve their goal.

In the early 1990's Mike Tyson was a formidable heavyweight prizefighter and essentially beat most of his opponents before they left the dressing room. In Tokyo, Tyson, with tons of firepower, encountered one James "Buster" Douglas several months after Douglas' mother passed away. In her passing, Douglas discovered a reservoir of strength and energy to face Tyson like no one had before. Tyson knocked him down early in the fight but Douglas rose to his feet and proceeded to absorb and dish out more punishment than Tyson was conditioned to take.

After capturing the heavyweight crown in defeating Tyson, Douglas faced Evander Holyfield who knocked Douglas to the canvas early in the fight. This time, Douglas lied there and ended the fight as the loser.

When asked about Douglas' loss in the Holyfield fight, one reporter remarked that Douglas could've won the fight if his mother would've come back to earth and died again; thus re-energizing his "will" to win.

"And Jesus said unto them, Because of your unbelief: for verily I say unto you, If ye have faith as a grain of mustard seed, ye shall say unto this mountain, Remove hence to yonder place; and it shall remove; and nothing shall be impossible unto you"

Matthew 17:20 KJV

CHAPTER FOUR
ENDANGERED SPECIES

In Case You Haven't Heard
By **SAKINA PITTS**: Public School Educator

There are so many issues facing high school youth today that it is very disheartening to see how many of them are surely on their way to being economically unstable citizens of this society. Some of the many challenges that I see our youth facing, especially in the urban environment include but not limited to:

- Gang violence
- Drug related issues
- Teen-aged pregnancy
- Lack of literacy
- Lack of technological opportunities
- Lack of religion/morality/spirituality

In my Newark New Jersey school district, GANG VIOLENCE is the most prominent issue that our youth face. They are consumed "24-7" with the latest gang "knowledge." It's so bad that even the students who would otherwise be uninterested in the "gang world" oftentimes feel pressured to succumb. They feel that even if they don't belong to one particular gang, per se, they must still be "in the know" due to "survival of the fittest."

We live in a day and age where our youth have NO fear of GOD and religion is forbidden in our schools. So where does that leave this younger generation? Babies are having babies and unable to care for them due to lack of resources and education, so the cycle just continues. Our streets are flooded with drugs, and the parents...who are not present in the schools and working with the teachers and/or administrators to move their children forward....are on drugs as well.

Our youth are NOT LITERATE! Many of them read far below their grade levels, and we ALL know that without literacy.....WE ARE TRULY LOST!!!!!

I feel that our youth are FAR LESS prepared for the real world today than they were 20 years ago. Americans, period, have declined globally in educational attainment and status. Other countries and cultures are proving to be more advanced and on the "cutting edge" of technology. With technology at its peak, we truly are not doing enough to create "real world" educational experiences for our youth so that they may in turn experience successes in the real world. These experiences have to be infused into the curricula that we follow and must also be supported by the parents of these children.

We haven't taken adequate time to "culture" our youth and give them the exposure that they need. We are not preparing them to become "critical thinkers" as well as "life long learners." I am PASSIONATE when it comes to the children that I service and those "who sit before me." Years ago, there was more accountability and even without technology being as prevalent as it is today, parents were concerned...teachers were concerned...the community was concerned. We believed in the notion "It takes a village..." We now have an *"Every man for himself"* approach that is only hurting our youth.

If I could change anything in the educational system process, it would be the NCLB (No Child Left Behind) laws that were put into effect by yet another politician who knows "everything" about education but has NOT taught a day in his "bloody" life !!!! Who are we fooling here? We have politician...after politician implementing law after law after law. Creating all of these federal and state mandates, but yet are not in the "trenches" with the children and do not sit down with educators and/or even parents for that matter when coming up with these "grand" failures of plans. So what happens? Teachers begin "teaching to the test" to ensure that the students pass all of these benchmarks and we truly lose sight of what is MOST important…..which is creating LIFE LONG LEARNERS WHO WILL ULTIMATELY REACH THE APEX OF THEIR EDUCATIONAL CAPACITIES IN HOPES OF BECOMING ECONOMICALLY AS WELL AS SOCIALLY STABLE CITIZENS OF THIS SOCIETY."

"GO FIGURE!!"

The Marginalization and Devastation of African-Descendant Males

"Sons are a heritage from the Lord, children a reward from him. Like arrows in the hands of a warrior are sons born in one's youth. Blessed is the man whose quiver is full of them. They will not be put to shame when they contend with their enemies in the gate"

Psalm 127:3-5 (NIV)

In case you didn't hear it the first time, "African American young men are under siege" (Harvey & Hill, 2004). According to statistics, they are suspended and expelled more than other students and they are filtered into special and alternative education programs more than other students (Harvey & Hill, 2004). Teen-aged black males have higher rates of detention and arrest and are incarcerated in juvenile and adult correctional facilities more than their peers (Harvey & Hill, 2004).

There has been a disproportionate arrest and confinement rate for African American males, according to The Coalition for Juvenile Justice (1996) since the 1960's (Drakeford, 2006). Despite these published reports the trend continues as minority juveniles (who are less than 6% of the total population) represented nearly 65% of those held in public facilities and 55% of those held in private facilities at the end of the last century (Drakeford & Staples, 2006).

The reason why the overrepresentation of black males in the prison systems is a critical factor for administrators, teachers, guidance counselors, and parents to understand is because the precursor to it is the overrepresentation of black males assigned to special education programs at an early school age; especially emotional and behavioral disorder programs (Drakeford & Staples, 2006).

Black youth experience differential treatment in the juvenile justice system in terms of confinement and release but also in the "structure of cumulative responses" and "revolving doors" (Drakeford & Staples, 2006).

There are multiple reasons why this continues to happen in such a free and equitable society. Some of the reasons are a) social, b) environmental c) institutional, and d) familial.

A SOCIAL CONTEXT: Where Bad Seems Good

As with all of the generations before them, today's youth have a propensity for engaging in "bad" behavior. Not always criminal, but the behavior is at the very least, anti-social and rebellious. Much of the anti-society behavior manifests in things like how they dress, talk and play.

Today there is a pervasive nuisance of youngsters (and some of their fathers) wearing their pants low enough for their underwear to be seen in public. "Saggin" (or "niggas" spelled backwards) is a relatively new social phenomenon that is sweeping the country faster than an Elvis Pressley record. For some odd reason, the boys in the hood and the boys in the 'burbs and now the boys in the *"sticks"* are of the mind that walking around with their britches showing is smooth and delightful. Some of the young brothers barely walk with their pants above their knees; holding them up with one hand as they walk around the block.

Well, legend has it that this "fashion" originated in one of two places: The Plantation or The Prison. It doesn't matter if it were either of them because they both represent something demonic to young black males.

On the plantation, slave owners would remove belts from the slaves, it is believed, to keep them from running away. Even then, young male slaves had enough dignity not to run around in their underwear; even if it meant their freedom from slavery. As they ran, their pants would fall down and they would hold them up with one hand so they could keep it moving. Needless to say, it would slow them down just enough for the posse to track them down.

In prisons, legend has it that males would walk around with their britches showing to alert other males that they were in an intimate relationship with another male. The dominant males would select their "bitch" or "property" and he would be off the market to the rest of the jail population.

If either of these is true, what creature in his right mind would want to voluntarily walk around like this in public? No omnipotent GOD would have his creation walking around like this either. Even in the Garden of Eden, as the BIBLE tells, man and woman hid themselves from GOD when they recognized their own nakedness. Unless it is a Victoria's Secret runway show, skimpy clothing and underwear are unsightly, unsanitary, vulgar and self-degrading based on the conventional norms of society...and therein lies the problem.

When the dominant culture in any society establishes the creed and behaviors for the underclass in their society, the underclass will occasionally defy the statutes and norms of the dominant class to symbolize independence from them. In essence, what is seen as "bad" by the dominant class can be viewed as "good" by the underclass. Although the saggin' fashion is visible in the suburbs and rural areas, its origin is widely believed to be from urban, inner-city areas. Other nonconformist attitudes are especially visible in schools. Good grades are viewed by many underclass youngsters as a bad thing (or a white thing). Profane language and substandard language becomes commonplace communication. Heck, sometimes the underclass creates its own language entirely (e.g. Ebonics, Pig Latin, etc.). Much of the debate about inequity in education is based on race because in America blacks are still viewed as an underclass population.

In the communities that are heavily populated by the underclass, it is sometimes viewed as a good thing to dress and act like a bad boy or bad girl. Reputations, street credibility and popularity result from the counter-culture actions of the inhabitants. "The streets" creates its own uniform standard of behavior, rules of engagement, and system of survival. One urban legend, Stanley Tookie" Williams was known for his aggressive and cutthroat style of street management. From behind bars, Williams said he finally "got it" and decided to turn his life around but it was too late for him because his deeds allowed someone else to decide whether he lived or died. The governor of the State of California pulled Williams' plug.

The sorcery and idolatry that many of our youth are participating in today is destroying them by the thousands.

Dying for "street cred" is foolish idolatry by any standards and means. Idolatry is so bad today, that young men and women are burglarizing and assaulting famous athletes and entertainers who are revered throughout society; including the inner-city neighborhoods. Over the past few years, Andre Blatche of the NBA Washington Wizards was shot during an apparent robbery, and numerous professional and college athletes have been gagged and bound (with their family members) in their homes while some young misguided souls sought to steal what these people spent all of their lives trying to earn. Darrent Williams of the NFL Denver Broncos was killed outside of a nightclub as he sat inside his limousine after his last game of the season (which ended up being the last game of his life).

However, it was the in-season murder of NFL Washington Redskins All-Pro Safety Sean Taylor that epitomized the struggles of the endangered species in modern day America.

Sean Taylor

Statistics speak to the majority of young black males dying at the hands of others between the ages of 19 and 24. Darrent Williams and Sean Taylor almost made it through the age of endangerment. They were both 24 years old.

Taylor's death sparked a huge controversy as media people and other players in the NFL talked about how his past antics finally caught up to him. They talked about how Taylor was fearful of his home environment in Florida and how so many young brothers and sisters did not like him because of his achievements and fortune. But that was before the truth of the incident unfolded.

Allegedly, four young men between the ages of 17 and 21 decided to drive over 100 miles from their hometown to break in Taylor's home. Little did they know that Taylor, his girlfriend and young daughter were sleeping in the house. It happened during the football season and no one expected Taylor to be there. By now most of you know the storylines but it is a scene that plays itself out all over America everyday: African American males dying at the hands of other African American males.

ENVIRONMENTAL CONTEXT: The Blame Game

Michael Eric Dyson, author and professor, and Bill Cosby, comedian and educator have offered their interpretations of the plight of the endangered species of black males (and blacks in general). Theirs is an ongoing debate over whether it is the system's fault or the people's fault. The debate continues over whether the government and corporate America should invest more in the development of black youth or whether black folks in endangered environments just need to pull themselves up by their own bootstraps.

Bishop T.D. Jakes in his book "Repositioning Yourself" gives a poignant account of how the life and times of black Americans could be interpreted. In it, Jakes describes a "two-headed coin" that has a head and a tail but still is the same coin. Neither side of the coin is right or wrong, just different sides. The coin (or the problem) is still the same.

In general, political pressure and judicial maneuvering can create a type of social change that improves the equity of African American students in all school settings (Smith & Kozleski, 2005). However, it is not uncommon for subordinate groups in every society, including Blacks in America, to have a collective fear and disdain for both the political and legal systems. This happens primarily because history proves that the political and legal systems are unfriendly toward subordinate groups who rarely access privilege and power because government and the judiciary won't allow it.

One advocate for the habilitation and strengthening of black communities nationwide is Captain Dennis Muhammad, founder of the ENOTA-ATONE project. Captain Dennis urges people to accept their contribution to the devastation and near demise of black men regardless of their race or socioeconomic standing.

For several years, Captain Dennis has provided training to community residents, youth, and law enforcement agencies to help them to bridge the gaps that impede positive growth and development of inner-city youth. In an article appearing by Andrea Muhammad in the Final Call (Nov. 3 2006), she discusses the possible impact programs like ENOTA can have on these communities:

"Founded by Dennis Muhammad, a captain in the Nation of Islam, ENOTA is a company that specializes in improving relationships between law enforcement and the communities they serve. In 2006, (the city of Detroit) announced a joint initiative with ENOTA to help both citizens and law enforcement take back their communities and stem the rising tide of crime." However, just after the partnership was announced, "the community was again rocked on Aug. 25 by the murder of 64-year-old activist and businessman Milton Goodson, the owner of Milts Gourmet Barbeque. He was fatally shot during a hold-up at his restaurant by a 16-year-old. The murder sent shockwaves through the community bringing expediency to the ENOTA Project…Capt. Dennis stressed that the 'Black community is at war with itself, thus experiencing civil war.'

- 2008 FCN Publishing, FinalCall.com

Adult Examples

Some of the behavior of our young black males is barbaric but we can't criticize the egg without examining the goose. Over the past few decades, adults participated in modern day idolatry in an intense desire to accumulate more and more "stuff." Black Americans who no longer had to sit at the back of the bus nor be denied access to the same stores as the dominant race, were committed to attaining the same level of education and opportunity as the dominant group; but also purchasing and acquiring material possessions at the same rate too. Many blacks learned to spend what they didn't have and take what wasn't theirs as they tried to keep pace with what they perceived as "White privilege."

During the past few decades, more and more Americans allowed "things" to dominate daily pursuits. They spent less time with family and more time working in an effort to raise their living standards. Specifically during the "Opulent 80's" when television shows like Dynasty and Dallas advertised an insatiable appetite and lust for riches, luxuries, and the neighbor's wife, the wealth gap grew wider and more embarrassing to this nation.

During these times, people lost some of their regard for the elders of the family and neighborhoods. Instead of the old lady on the stoop being concerned about our kids, she was viewed as "nosey." We started to disrespect our elders and each other at work and on the roads. We grooved to the tunes of "Me & Mrs. Jones" and "Superfly"; one about an adulterous and the other about a pimp/pusher (and that was primarily

Black folks). The rest of America was getting busted for insider trading and movies like the "Godfather" made heroes of scoundrels and vagabonds. The pursuit of wealth and power led to skyrocketing credit card debt and public officials set bad examples by "Watergating" their way into power.

By the time crack cocaine hit the "New Jack" cities, followed by the emergence of the world wide web, at-risk youth were by-products of adult greed and lawlessness and jack-legged, hypocritical religious leaders. We either were so busy raising our standard of living, jumping in/out of bed, or selling/doing so much dope that our kids were raising themselves. On a systemic level, as the "War on Drugs" and stricter academic requirement continued over the last 2 decades, violent acts were committed more frequently and by younger offenders; mostly killing other young people (Webber, 1997).

ADD—Absent Dad Disorder

"Fathers, provoke not your children to anger, lest they be discouraged"
Colossians 3:21

A pastor in Maryland once told his congregation of a story about the elephants who lived in a certain area of Africa. Contradictory to "natural selection", the elephants were attacking the rhinoceros in droves. Apparently, elephants are no more a natural predator of rhinoceros as Black men are of one another, yet the elephants were suddenly wreaking havoc against their mammal brethren.

According to the story, researchers traced this unnatural behavior to one isolated series of events in that part of Africa. The kings of the prior generations had killed many adult elephants to cut off and sell their tusks. Therefore, the practice left many "orphaned" elephants alone to raise themselves. The result: The baby elephants, now grown, didn't have sense enough not to attack the rhinoceros because no one was around to teach them who their real enemies were in their habitat.

Over three-fourths of children showing behavioral disorders have no father in the home according to the Centers for Disease Control (CDC) (Stephens 2007). Additional data indicate that fatherless children are 32 times more likely to run away from home and 10—20 times more likely to commit rape, become substance abusers and wind up imprisoned.

Too many young black boys are raising themselves without a father in their home or even worse, in their lives. Too many young black girls are being raised without a father in their home or worse yet, in their lives. For those who have worked in the center of the city or in the sprawling upper class suburbs, the same trend exists in both: Sixty-six percent of black children in America do not have a traditional nuclear family in the home for a variety of reasons and this reality does not change much with the rise of the socioeconomic level of the black family.

Disappearing Male Muscle

In today's business models, there is less of a need and emphasis on physical strength and agility. Even though there is a burgeoning trend toward physical fitness and improved health and nutrition, the need for physical strength and agility in the workplace is rapidly dwindling as America and the rest of the world moves further away from an agrarian and industrial society.

As a result, tomorrow's business model has a premium on intellectual capacity and has begun to devalue physical strength. Consequently (and quite appropriately I might add), America's secondary and higher education schools are raising the academic bar to prepare its citizens for tomorrow's business needs. In high schools and college campuses across the nation, we are noticing the disappearing of "Male Muscle."

In times past, male muscle was a necessity on the farm and in the fields. As women tended to the needs of the offspring and maintained the home environment, men were required to hunt, fish, farm, and skin in order to feed and clothe the family. Of course, the women participated in these endeavors too, but it was the male that was most often called upon to trap and subdue dinner. Also during this time in American history, the African male was frequently raised as "chattel" to do plantation work to benefit the economy of slave traders and owners.

As America moved into the industrial age of machinery, men were required to build the railroads and operate heavy equipment and machinery. During this time, several contact and collision recreational activities were developed. Basketball, football, baseball, hockey and the Native American sport of lacrosse provided young males with the "exercise" needed to develop the agility and strength for farm, field, and industrial work.

As America transitioned into the "automation" age, smaller machines were created that could handle more work in faster time. Communication, food processing, clothing designs, etc. were easier and faster to execute. America was less dependent on "muscle" and more dependent on "innovation."

Sports then became an integral part of the young male experience because boys weren't doing the hard labor tasks of their fathers. The African Descendant males who no longer were slave labor became an essential element in "sports labor."

In today's America, females are as integrated in sports, by law, as the males. On high school and college campuses nationwide, we are noticing an increase in "female muscle" as male muscle decreases. Much of the male muscle is now going to prison because too many males are unwilling or unequipped to navigate in the modern business model. Too few young males are involved in sports because they are either hanging out on the street corner or have no interest in competitive athletics.

Furthermore, the new business model in secondary education is creating an "either—or" scenario for school administrators. Either they commit to building highly competitive male sports or they don't. Football is the sport that causes the biggest dilemma on high school campuses.

Football consumes more resources than any other scholastic sport. It costs the most money, has the most injuries, and requires the most time. It also engages more students than any other sport. A typical high school football program will have 60-80 male players. It costs approximately $500 to outfit one football player for practices and games. Football typically engages more "male muscle" than any other sport. As the male muscle disappears, so does football…and vice versa.

INSTITUTIONAL CONTEXT: Institutionalized Segregation

Lesson # 6:

When at-risk, troubled, criminally-minded black male youth are sent to detention centers and correctional facilities, they more likely become at-risk, troubled, criminally-minded black male adults. When at-risk, troubled, criminally-minded black male youths are sent to high-quality, strict-disciplined, *college-oriented academic institutions instead of prisons (and they are patient with them), they eventually adapt and become productive, family-oriented, high-achieving black male adults. It costs $30,000-$50,000 per year to send them to correctional facilities...It costs $10,000-$15,000 to send them to a McNamara or DeMatha High School.*

American educational systems are viewed by most people as a way of leveling the field for all people regardless of race, creed, or color. In order to achieve this equality, American leaders thought it best to reduce the amount of segregation (separation by race, creed or color) in our nation's schools. Racial segregation is a cornerstone of the American legacy from the days of slavery to the present-day "legally enforced segregation of public and private institutions..." Although there are many examples of integrated schools where black and white children co-educate on a daily basis, it is more the exception than the norm (Smith & Kozleski, 2005).

What is most disturbing is that many of those schools that are integrated continue to have segregated practices as evidenced by "students of color being more likely to (a) be placed in special education, (b) fail to graduate; and (c) take vocational rather than college preparatory courses" (Smith & Kozleski, 2005). In addition, fewer black and brown students excel on the standardized tests (ACT/SAT) and have less access to a competitive academic curriculum in their home school (Smith & Kozleski, 2005).

In every society there are established levels of power that include a "dominant group" and "subordinate groups." The dominant group maintains leverage and power by "keeping subordinates in their designated places" by marginalizing and "othering" members of the subordinate classes. In education,

"Othering" is when students are placed in alternative programs within integrated educational settings to reduce the risk of the perceived dangers they pose to their fellow students (Smith & Kozleski, 2005). For example, large for their age black males between the ages of 5-7 are more likely to be identified as at-risk, special education and/or disciplinary problems in integrated grade schools. By "labeling" them as such, they can be removed from the mainstream academic tracks and placed in "alternative" settings; which ultimately means they will interact less with the rest of the children in their grade levels. Othering and marginalization continues to occur in adult corporate, academic and civic organizations.

One example of such is the overwhelming number of large black adult males with college degrees in education who are limited to working primarily in athletics and alternative programs in secondary schools.

Ethics, power, and privilege are connected and affect all aspects of the educational system. They are "particularly insidious" in teaching, course development, teacher preparation, policy development, and decision making in local schools (Smith & Kozleski, 2005).

Institutional Intervention

How do we orient tomorrow's African-American male youth toward achievement today? Of all the approaches and strategies out there, none will work without consistent and persistent intervention done at EVERY level of a black males' youth cycle; or the potential for their academic/career achievement dwindles.

Whether it is mentoring & counseling, faith-based, aggression reduction/conflict resolution, social skills training, or career development education, it has to be a mainstay in their lives until and throughout their college careers (Harvey & Hill, 2004). It is advisable for each intervention unit to have after-school and/or weekend components, family development, and "individual and family counseling" strategies to enhance their viability (Harvey & Hill, 2004). It costs time, energy and money. The powers that be don't seem to mind the amount of time and energy invested in black youth but appear to have serious issue with the amount of money that needs to be invested. Yet those same powers are much more willing and able to spend $50,000 per year to incarcerate a black male youth compared to a fraction of that cost to educate him.

In fact, it costs less to send a troubled youth to a major university than it does to send him to prison. That is a wonderful strategy to consider: A case study where we send troubled black males in the death range (19-24 years old) to the local community college instead of prison. At the local community college, they'll develop skills that they can use anywhere in society. At the state prison, they're more likely to develop an attitude that will "re-incarcerate" them in the future.

The McNamara/DeMatha Lesson

Bishop McNamara High School is a private Catholic college-preparatory school in Forestville, Maryland (Prince George's County). Grimes graduated from McNamara when it was a single-sex school. Grimes, like many of his black male peers struggled with the racial overtones of the school at the time and also struggled with the strict disciplinary code of conduct at the school.

Bevill attended DeMatha Catholic High School in Hyattsville, Md. with very similar demographics. He encountered some of the same conditions seen at McNamara.

Lesson # 1: The first lesson for a black male student at McNamara/DeMatha in the 1980's was detention was held after-school and on Saturdays. Upon visiting detention, it was plain to see that nearly 60% of the students detained were black at both schools at a time when their black population was about twenty-thirty percent.

Lesson # 2: The majority of the black males in both schools were involved in athletics either by default (because they like to play sports) or by design (they were recruited to play sports).

Lesson # 3: McNamara/DeMatha graduates went to college. The white ones, the black ones and the red ones went to college when they graduated. Vocational, military, trade schools weren't even a topic of discussion.

Lesson # 4: Many of the black males had a very hard time adapting to the rules and regulations of the school.

Lesson # 5: Most of the black males learned to adjust and adapt to the rules. Most of them graduated and went on to college or the military and are successful and productive U.S. citizens today. Some of their career fields include medicine, education, real estate, law enforcement, technology, entertainment, law and athletics...And we're not talking subordinate roles either. Many of them are running the joint.

How did this happen?

Simple!

Instead of sending some of the troubled black males to reform school for bad-ass kids, the community, the parents, and the school itself came up with some money and sent them to "reform college preparatory" school…Bishop McNamara/DeMatha High School.

Lesson # 6: When at-risk, troubled, criminally-minded black male youth are sent to detention centers and correctional facilities, they more often become at-risk, troubled, criminally-minded black male adults. When at-risk, troubled, criminally-minded black male youths are sent to high-quality, strict-disciplined, college-oriented academic institutions instead (and they are patient with them), they eventually adapt and become productive, family-oriented, high-achieving black male adults. It costs $30,000-$50,000 per year to send them to correctional facilities…It costs $10,000-$15,000 to send to McNamara or DeMatha High school.

This is not to say that the DeMatha's and McNamara's of the world are able to enroll a large percentage of at-risk, troubled, criminally-minded black male youth. In fact, the opposite is true.

However, the lesson is the same, somewhere out there in our vast society, we can create high-quality, strict-disciplined, college-oriented academic institutions that can accommodate these young black males. Since we are able to build and fund the prisons each year, a slight strategic shift in how the government spends black folks' tax dollars would accomplish this feat with absolute expediency.

The Level Playing Field

Across the board, black adults in America have come to understand that the nation's system of democracy is not a level playing field for black people. True or not, it is their perception based on past history and modern day events in this country.

For today's black male youth, there are more mechanisms to compete on equal footing with the rest of American society than ever. The question is: What will it take for more black males to utilize these tools to further their cause?

Technology is one of the tools which help black youth to keep pace with the academic requirements in school. The "virtual" nature of computer and internet based learning can be a solution to the very educational inequities experienced by many inner-city and rural black males. Computer-based instruction can be used to overcome geographic limitations, lack of school resources, race/ethnicity bias, and substandard teaching (Blaylock & Newman, 2005).

The increased role of mentors and support groups for young black males helps them navigate through society. Support groups, different from a therapeutic treatment model delivered by professional psychologists, emphasizes the strengths and abilities of its participants (Wright & McCreary, p. 48). They encourage black males to utilize their tools and talents to achieve their goals and overcome roadblocks. This recognition and encouragement creates "a self-identification of assets that are meaningful and valuable" (Wright & McCreary, p. 48).

Athletics and the Black Male

Athletics is probably the quintessential "level playing field" for young black males, which is one of the reasons why so many seem to excel in that arena. Yet golf governors have tried to "Tiger-proof" golf courses, the NCAA outlawed dunking when Lew Alcindor (Kareem Abdul-Jabbar) was in college, and Olympian Jesse Owens raced horses instead of men.

Sports competition in its purest form means that everyone plays by the same rules and money, race, gender, or religious belief don't matter. If it's raining on my side of the field, it's raining on yours. If it's sunny on your side it's sunny on mine. The referees are supposed to be neutral and everybody has the same equipment and number of players on each side.

Because very little else in society is a level playing field, young black males usually enjoy and commit to sports. Young black males have a completely different experience on the playing field than anywhere else in society. There they can be assertive, forthright, and risky without being sent to detention or suspended. Sports provide young black males with a safe-haven that allows them to be freer to be who they want to be.

Objective vs the Subjective

The reason athletics is such a great place for young black males has more to do with sociology than talent or ability. In human relationships, most decisions and opportunity are made based on objective or subjective criteria.

Subjective criteria decisions and opportunity are formed by people's perceptions. Perceptions are like opinions and everybody has them. Unfortunately for young black males, society's perception of them (especially among the dominant group) is based on the stereotypes presented by media, history books, and racist ideologists. Those stereotypes are "rigid, negative, and grossly inaccurate" (McCreary & Wright, p. 26). The stereotypes feed a negative bias toward black males which builds those negative perceptions to make educators, business leaders, and elected officials less inclined to support black males' goals and desires.

Objective criteria are less about perceptions and more about "standardization." In basketball, football, and now golf, African-American males are setting and meeting those standards while raising them daily. Objective decision-making leads those in charge to look at everyone the same and focus on specific results instead of opinions. Measurable results such as test scores, game scores, and yards per carry are not abstract numbers; they are justifiable, documented, and irrefutable (steroids and cheating notwithstanding).

Just to highlight the importance and significance of objective versus subjective criteria decision-making, let's take a look at Japan as a model. During World War II the Japanese were enemies of America. To signal the end of World War II, the U.S. did something in Japan that had never been done before and to date has never been done since: They dropped two nuclear/atomic bombs on the country.

After the war ended, the Japanese who were interested in making their way in the world realized that the most powerful country in the nation (USA) did not think very highly of the Japanese and would probably not want to do business with them. Somewhere along the way the Japanese people recognized their assets such as self-discipline and focus were a useful commodity to the world. They decided to base much of their academy on Math and Science (predominantly math). They realized that math was more of an absolute that was based on objective, measurable data. Aligned with math were fields such as accounting, engineering, architecture, and medicine. These fields of study are known as "terminal" degrees.

On the other hand, they also realized that "humanities" was a discipline that offered them little hope to compete globally. Many of them felt that education, sociology, psychology and social work were far too subjective for them to gain respect from Americans. They envisioned Americans not wanting to "hear" what they have to say...so they stopped talking. And if you haven't noticed, they still don't do much talking.

The classroom became their laboratory and math was their ticket. Every structural design from roads to computers required a mathematical interest and the Japanese were prepared to make their deposit.

Less than 40 years later, the Japanese had become one of the strongest economic and industrial forces in the world and whether Americans wanted to deal with them or not, Americans needed their mathematical skills to successfully move into the 21st century. The Japanese didn't care about being seen or heard. They provided much of the "backbone" of support and most of us didn't know they even worked in our companies. They made themselves a necessity to the most powerful nation in the world.

America never invested the same kind of resources in black Americans that it did in the Japanese. After the atom bombs were dropped, parts of Japan looked like third world underdeveloped nations, but their schools quickly regenerated into cutting edge monoliths of higher academia (significantly aided by the USA). Their third graders were studying at par with some of America's inner-city and rural tenth graders. Japanese kids were getting educated as black American kids were trying to overcome.

As more black male youth grew frustrated with their academic experience, their athletic experience grew to new heights as the television became a household necessity. Black Americans had finally discovered their "terminal" value to America and the rest of the world. Not mathematics, not science, not education...football! (in other words, entertainment).

After hurricane Katrina hit the gulf states, former First Lady Barbara Bush said it best as she stroked a young black boys' head to reassure him that despite the horror of the storm and the disruption it would cause his family, he would still be "a great basketball player someday."

SPECIAL REPORT
ON THE POSITIVE SIDE

"And ye shall eat in plenty, and be satisfied, and praise the name of the LORD
your GOD, that he dealt wondrously with you: and my people shall never be ashamed"

Joel 2:26 NIV

Same as it Ever Was?

The U.S. Presidential election process of 2008 has revealed some stunning psych-social shifts in the hearts and minds of Americans. It is obvious that the world wide web, cable television and cellular phones has given more people an opportunity to see and hear things that they may never have seen or heard before the technological boom.

In tomorrow's world, people are becoming less afraid of the "what" and the "who" they don't know because ordinary people now have access to some of the same information that was available only to the privileged few in the past. In tomorrow's world, children can be freed from the fear of "stranger danger" that was taught in American schools and homes for 100 years; thereby, making us more reluctant to meet new people as children and subsequently as adults. In tomorrow's world, kids are able to snap a photo of a curious stranger and his/her license plates with their cellphone and email it directly to law enforcement.

Tomorrow's children are going to be more interactive with people throughout the world. Today the fortunes of MySpace, Facebook and the like are displacing large, archaic multinational corporations on Wall Street by selling of all things: Opportunities for new RELATIONSHIPS. These online services may not be driving our desire to interact with others as much as reflecting our desire to interact with others.

2008 Presidential primary candidates were raising more money in a shorter time because of the web. For the first time ever, there was a woman and a Black man offering serious contention to a field historically owned by dominant culture men. For the first time, people are publicly embracing others unlike them and it sends a clear message that Americans are becoming more respectful of our differences.

To the Future and Beyond

Although it is reported that 1 in 100 Americans are behind prison bars (www.soulofsyracuse.com, March 2008) prisons can be restructured to provide academic and skill training instead of just "warehousing" inmates. Then we may see a decline in the number of repeat offenders in the future. If prisoners can leave jail with the hope that if they straighten up and fly right they can not only survive but excel in society, they will be more equipped to endure the challenges and adversity awaiting them.

On the positive side, the Chocolate Cities are turning browner and whiter. On the positive side, the suburbs are turning darker and blacker. At some point during this transition some of the whites will get stuck in the suburbs and some of the blacks will get stuck in the cities; then they will be forced to deal with each other as neighbors. As a matter of fact, the housing crisis of the late 2000's is doing just that to families across the nation who want to "Archie Bunker" or "George Jefferson" their way to segregating themselves based on race or class; ultimately handicapping their own children who can't afford to have their parents' fears and prejudices injected into their emotions.

Some day soon we may actually get to the point where we will no longer feel the need to "voluntarily" segregate ourselves based on race and ethnicity because we no longer have to fear "strangers" and the "bogeyman."

In the Parliament-Funkadelic worlds of communication, there is a concept called, *"Same as it ever was."* It simply means that nothing really changes but just shifts, slides, and morphs into a different form.

But something's changing in the air. Suddenly today there is less of the same as it ever was. Or at least it looks like that day of change for black males is nearer than it ever was.

Academic Parity = From At-Risk to "At-Promise"

African American males are more readily identified in terms of their failures than their outstanding achievements (Thompson & Lewis, 2005). In spite of all of the negative rhetoric about black male youth there are other aspects of their growth, development and performance that can be celebrated. A case study of an African American male growing up in the Baltimore area sheds some light on their ability to compete in rigorous academic curricula.

In the study, the subject petitioned his school administrator to offer an advanced pre-calculus/calculus course in his school which offered honors Algebra II as its terminal mathematics course. He offered a compelling argument and supported it with his own record of 1130 on the SAT and a 3.4 gpa, making him the 7th highest ranked student in his class (Thompson & Lewis, 2005).

Furthermore, his efforts and achievements underscored the fact that African American students were very interested in mathematics but the unavailability of advanced courses prohibited them from aspiring to a higher level of coursework (Thompson & Lewis, 2005). This evidence speaks to the fact that students can and will only aspire to the highest level of achievement presented to them in an academic setting. In order for them to reach higher expectations they have to see a pathway to getting there.

Self and Peers—Positive & Healthy

"Be of good courage, and he shall strengthen your heart, all ye that hope in the LORD"

Psalm 31:24 NIV

Schools are more aware of the need to teach students to recognize potentially dangerous situations and adapt to them accordingly. Educators are being asked to help students to develop self-management skills to make them more proactive learners and gain feelings of self-worth (Gable, et al, 2005). When students believe they are worthy to stand for something then they won't just fall for anything.

As classmates are coached to praise appropriate peer behavior and ignore disruptive peer behavior they send a clear message to each other about peer accepted behavior (Gable, et al, 2005); which is as powerful as meeting adult behavior expectations. When youngsters (especially females) start turning away from guys with their pants hanging down to their knees, the guys will stop wearing their pants around their knees. As youth hold each other more accountable, it will have a healthy and positive impact on their overall development.

Health and intellect are two very important qualities for youth to have in order to succeed in our educational systems (Scales, 2000). American government, schools, parents, and children are currently engaging in an all-out war against unhealthy lifestyles and nutritional choices. Over time, the effects of a sustained effort to improve the well-being of our children will manifest itself in very positive ways. Furthermore, these efforts will alter our children's attitudes and perceptions to the extent that they will sponsor healthy choices with their future children.

Based on a variety of research, educators are aware of the importance of the health improvement and intellectual development of students. The research concludes that children who are healthy in mind, body and spirit are more likely to attend school regularly, present fewer occurrences of deviant behavior, and are better prepared for life after high school (Scales, 2000).

Although there is an ongoing preoccupation with dealing with drug/alcohol abuse and violence in our schools, precipitated by funding opportunities and school shootings at Columbine High and other places, other aspects of school/students health are gaining more attention. School-connectedness is now being viewed as a critical element in resolving and preventing unhealthy choices and violence in our schools (Scales, 2000). As students feel a greater sense of fair treatment at school and feel closer to their peers and educators (Resnick et al. 1997), they are better able to handle anxiety/depressive episodes, feelings of aggression, and increased urges to engage in sexual intercourse (Scales, 2000).

Some believe that a student's sense of belongingness has more of an affect on student health than the school environment itself or classroom size and diversity.

A Minneapolis based organization, Search Institute, collected data on more than one million schoolchildren in 1,000 communities and discovered students' connectedness is a prime factor in their long-term health and success (Scales, 2000).

In addition, schools are concentrating more and more on the "developmental assets" of youth at different stages of growth to enhance their chances to succeed. Positive peer relationships (Leffert et al., 1998), self-management, self-discipline, self-restraint, etc., effective problem/conflict resolutions, quality of home life, and school participation are developmental assets which help youth to shun at-risk/anti-social behavior (Scales, 2000). These developmental assets generally apply to students who refuse to use forbidden substances, engage in pre-marital sex, control their temper, and adjust well to the challenges and pressures of performing in class and other school-related programs (Scales, 2000).

In terms of developmental assets which promote overall school success (e.g. a spirit of volunteering, delayed gratification and overcoming adversity), engagement in co-curricular activities, cultural relevance and competence, positive self-perception, organization and management, and reading and homework as a form of recreation are primary goals to help students to excel in their school environment.

Many researches also point to a relatively underutilized resource within our schools: the support staff of guidance counselors, psychologists, social workers, deans of students, and coaches as interdisciplinary "care teams" of school adults who can relate more deeply to students from a personal and career perspective.

As we move forward to continue the work to build stronger schools and students, the enhancement of these "developmental assets" will help to define (or at least refine) tomorrow's youth. The hope is that more of them will spend significant time in organized after-school programs, learn to get along with and seek to understand peers of different race and ethnicity, and develop better planning and decision-making skills. Eventually, they shall build a stronger academic work ethic and build relationships with other adults who take a keen interest in them. Hopefully they will read and write more for fun (instead of spending a counterproductive amount of time in Facebook/MySpace/Play Station), exhibit stronger internal character and positive external behavior, and help their peers to do the same (Scales, 2000).

Technology

The internet is a powerful tool and is more accessible to everyone. Most people can access it at work, school and the public library. The World Wide Web lets people buy things without going to the store, get information on just about any topic without going to the library, and make long-distance phone calls with no extra charge (Blaylock & Newman, 2005).

Computers can deliver instruction to anyone regardless of location, age, race, sex or income level. Computer-based instruction offers underrepresented students the same college preparation courses and career exposure that were available only to well-funded urban, suburban and private schools in the past (Blaylock & Newman, 2005). Technology is starting to displace textbooks (Blaylock & Newman, 2005) and audio-visual equipment in schools, reducing space and cost, and improving efficiency and flexibility.

K-16 Schooling

The disconnect between higher education and secondary schools often leave parents and students confused and frustrated about how to get into college (Gilroy, 2003).

The historical relationship between K-12 secondary and higher education institutions has been a disjointed one. There is a new call for more collaboration between the two systems to help raise academic standards, improve teacher preparation, and enhance community involvement (Gilroy, 2003).

College professors usually distance themselves from secondary instructors but more University Deans and professors are interested in joining forces with K-12 schools in their neighboring communities. One such endeavor, the Maryland Partnership for Teaching and Learning K-16 is creating end-of-course exams for high school seniors. The program is also working to improve high school students' writing and comprehension skills, creating more teachers to handle the eventual exodus of baby-boomer educators, and trying to improve the training of teachers to handle the complex world of urban education (Gilroy, 2003). Another program sees Temple University and the Philadelphia School District try to increase the number of certified middle-school teachers from diverse backgrounds (Gilroy, 2003).

A consortium of 42 higher education networks has surfaced in Philadelphia as Drexel, University of Pennsylvania, and Penn State act as permanent anchors to support improved neighborhoods and schools. As higher education builds working relationships with secondary school systems, many people are optimistic of its benefits to the total community (Gilroy, 2003).

Similar efforts are going on around the country. In California, Stanford University is pushing for states to raise minimum high school graduation requirements to be compatible with more competitive college entrance requirements (Gilroy, 2003). The disconnect between higher education and secondary schools often leave parents and students confused and frustrated about how to get into college (Gilroy, 2003). Compound those frustrations with a single-parent, bullet-riddled neighborhood and it stands to reason why many inner-city students fail to perceive they are college material.

Between the year 2000-2010 estimates indicate there will be over 20 million new teacher hires in the U.S. Typically the new teacher hires are white middle-class females, many of whom prefer teaching white middle-class students in the suburbs (Medina, et al, 2005). A number of them will take teaching jobs in lower-income urban school districts with an increasingly diverse student body. The push has begun to train these teachers to teach in these schools as well as certify more racial minority teachers to work in these settings (Medina, et al, 2005).

Turning the perception of at-risk youth into "at-promise" students means the teachers are learning how to understand and address diversity in the classroom. It is no longer enough to just focus on the social issues of parenting, violence, and incarceration without teachers making an all-out effort to combat the ill-effects within the classroom to raise student achievement levels. Teachers aren't expected to be effective in these settings unless they examine their own personal attitudes, belief systems and cultural perceptions (Medina, et al, 2005) which creep into their teaching style.

The shift from focusing on how teachers teach to how students learn (Linek, et al, 2003) offers promising hope for all youth moving forward.

Distress vs. "Eustress"

Distress frequently happens as a result of an event or condition that appears to be out of one's control. Eustress is caused by a decision one makes to pursue an event or condition as part of a goal within one's control...

All stress is not the same. There is a fundamental difference between distress and "eustress." According to the online reference, wikepedia, distress is the most commonly-referred to type of stress, having negative implications, whereas eustress is a positive form of stress, usually related to desirable events in a person's life. Both can be equally taxing on the body, and are cumulative in nature, depending on how well a person adapts to the cause of the stress.

Distress caused by personal and professional conditions is difficult for any human being to handle regardless of age. It's what makes Britney Spears, a multimillionaire songstress, slip into drug or alcohol binges and exhibit erratic and seemingly uncontrollable behavior; endangering the welfare of herself and her family. The same kind of distress which may have caused actress Anna Nicole Smith to slip into depression so deep it literally caused her to take her own life by overusing medication.

Economic or financial distress in America is one of the most prolific stressors in modern day society. One of the leading causes of divorce is due to financial strain. In addressing this situation, consultants are developing therapeutic treatment for financial exorcism.

Understanding and managing financial matters is so important to human beings that the practice needs to begin as early in life as possible. People benefit from 'family" financial training and counseling because financial issues directly or indirectly affect every member of the household.

In recognizing the stress of growing up in our society for tomorrow's youth today, it is best to engage youth in programs which create eustress instead of distress. Eustress is the kind of stress that causes us to move toward a goal whereas distress is the kind of stress that causes us to move away from the situation. Distress frequently happens as a result of an event or condition that appears to be out of one's control, leading to heightened anxiety and fear. Eustress is caused by a decision one makes to pursue an event or condition as part of a goal within one's control and creates positive tension and anticipation instead of anxiety and depression.

In capturing the essence of eustress, Coach Bryce Bevill and his supporters have developed a series of workshops, camps and seminars on various industry conditions which youth are sure to encounter in their lifetimes. These training camps and programs are part of his "TOTAL FOCUS" on youth development. One unique theorem he addresses is that parents and children rarely learn in simultaneous environments, furthering the misunderstandings and misperceptions between them. If parents and children can educate themselves about anything together it can build bridges and cooperation between them.

These camps and training sessions can also build bridges between educators, coaches, businesspersons and parents, thus connecting historically divergent interests of society. By taking an inventory of the interests, skills, and professional expertise of parents and local stakeholders, Bevill's training concept maximizes on the local resources of any community to further the character, discipline, education, and capacity of not only the pupil but the trainer as well. Just like in effective mentoring programs there is a reciprocal benefit to the learner and the teacher. They develop mutual trust and dependability and everyone benefits from the powerful networking universe that the formal and informal exchange of ideas offers.

Among the industry topics people recommend are:

> Etiquette
> Property Ownership & Management
> Safety & Security
> Transferable Skills
> Organization & Management
> Financial Discipline
> Health and Nutrition
> Cultural Sensitivity
> Relationship Sensitivity

Because so many of these topics intertwine at various points, Bevill sees the need for an interdisciplinary training model that can be used by any industry. For example, he is working with a coach and personal trainer to offer "speed" camps to growing athletes. But within this speed camp is a component that deals with nutrition, thus offering a "speed and nutrition" camp that can be utilized by young athletes in soccer, volleyball, baseball, gymnastics, track, football, basketball, hockey, cheerleading and field hockey. The extemporaneous value of this camp is more students will discover that they have the basics to participate in more than one sport, which obviously helps the coaches and school all the way around. The more activities youth engage in, the better their attendance, the stronger the school spirit, and the less they get into trouble.

Re-Entering Society

In 1838 the Pennsylvania Supreme Court made it legal to remove children from their residence and place them in institutions when they engaged in criminally deviant behavior.

The first juvenile court is believed to have been started in Chicago, Illinois and it operated on the children's behalf. At the time, the courts' emphasis was on treatment/rehabilitation (Binder, 1988) instead of imprisonment/punishment (Granello & Hanna, 2003). As the decades went by, there has been a tremendous increase in the number of adolescents imprisoned (Smith, 1998) or involved in the criminal justice system (Granello & Hanna, 2003).

The rise in juvenile imprisonment is a direct result of the change in states' philosophy from rehabilitation to punishment. An increase in sexual and physical abuse of adolescents in correctional facilities is the unwanted side-effects of the punishment philosophy. Incidents of adolescent suicide due to the lack of counseling provisions and jail overcrowding are also caused by the transition toward juvenile punishment from juvenile treatment (Granello & Hanna, 2003).

Youth, while they are in jail and after they are released, need substantive counseling programs to help them to turn away from at-risk and criminal behavior in the future. In the Journal of Counseling and Development (2003), The Ohio State University scholar Paul Granello and Fred Hanna of Johns Hopkins University, write, "There is a critical need for counselors and other human service professionals to formulate a viable approach to the treatment of adolescents who are involved with the juvenile justice system. However, many counselors and mental health professionals choose to avoid working with these populations given their legal involvement, emotional and behavioral volatility, resistance to treatment, and multiple problems (Hanna, Hanna, & Keys, 1999)."

School and Rehabilitation Counselors among others are probably in a better position to aid in incarcerated youths' personal progress than law enforcement. Due to the systemic and volatile nature of incarceration, a collaborative effort among law enforcement personnel and the helping professions is advisable. Counselors and mental health professionals are trained to use empathic responses to juvenile needs and problems whereas law enforcement may not have the liberty to be as patient and hospitable. The overall goals and objectives of the counselors and mental health agents must include helping youth to modify their perceptions, expectations and assessment of aggressive/violent situations if they are going to become assimilated and productive members of American society (Granello & Hanna, 2003).

Connecting or re-connecting incarcerated youth to the larger communities is an extremely important treatment paradigm. It is essential to the reinstatement of adolescents from disenfranchised, oppressed minority groups. Counselors and mental health workers have to be aware of the landscape of the communities they re-enter and the services accessible to them in times of need or the chances of youthful offenders successfully migrating into general society is nil.

On Point for College

Practically every student will go to work, go into the military, or go to college after completing high school. Some will actually choose to do nothing but lie on their Mama's sofa until they find themselves…but this choice we do not recommend.

Attending college means different things to different people and we decided to submit a brief Q&A for our readers from some of our villagers as they give feedback on higher education:

Pamela Chisley

Did you attend college?
Yes, a community college.

Why did you choose the college you attended?
Due to the uncertainty of what my career goals were at that time. I previously thought that I wanted to be a beautician and I followed that career interest the last 3 years of high school. Once I graduated from high school, I followed that dream for about 2 years and decided that it wasn't what I wanted to do for the rest of my life/career so I took some clerical and business classes at the community college (trying to find myself). Later, I enrolled in Washington School for Secretaries for their 6 month training class. I graduated then started my clerical trail in the government. Now 23 years later, I am a Manager/Supervisory Human Resources Specialist (Chief of my section) that deals with grievances and arbitrations. I have a staff of four.

Did the college experience meet your expectations?
At that time it did.

Charles Gilbert

Did you attend college? **Yes**

Why did you choose the college you attended?
Undergraduate internship opportunities and on-campus interviews for permanent placement

Did the college experience meet your expectations?
Definitely

Gilbert B. Hoffman

Did you go to college?

I attended The University of Maryland. I was offered a football scholarship and of course, accepted. My major was English Literature. There were no other athletes majoring in English at the time. Many majored in Physical Education or Law Enforcement. My advisor told me that English would prepare me for law school.

I loved the social life at U of M. I also met other students from all walks of life. Many had part-time jobs or were newlyweds and were planning to start their families. Marriage was not at all in my college plans. I was a full-time student athlete and my job was football. I spent 40 hours a week doing something football related. I lived with other football players and socialized with people who loved to be around football or at least around football players.

Did the college experience meet your expectations?

The great part about college was the independence. Besides my football obligations it was great living on my own, especially since it was paid for. Visiting with friends at 2 a.m. was almost commonplace. Lots of interesting things go on at 2 a.m.

Saturdays during football season were the best. The competition, the crowd, the hype in general was almost indescribable. Everyone treated you like some sort of celebrity. It was great. Our football team had winning seasons back then and we always went to a prestigious post-season bowl game. Those were some fun years.

Alternatives of Higher Ed

Every student will not be able to finish high school and go straight to a four year college. Some will go right to work while others may go into the military. Still others will both work and go to school and many of them head over to the local community college to obtain a two year degree.

American community colleges are known for providing advanced degree opportunities for underserved, nontraditional students. Community colleges give people the chance to work on technical or vocational skills while they are in school or working (Handel, 2007).

Despite the advantages and benefits the community colleges offer students, they have historically been looked upon as a second-class citizen of the higher education environment. They often have to compete with secondary schools and private small schools for funding and students. There has always been a distant and unenthusiastic view of community colleges among four year college professors because they know that many of the community college students lack the prerequisite academic skill for acceptance into four year schools (Handel, 2007).

Students who are academically disadvantaged find it more difficult to earn the standard 4 year degree and choose the community college route and transfer to 4 year schools later. For many years, educators have worried about the small numbers who make the transition successfully. Fifty-percent of the community-college students who plan to transfer eventually succeed at completing the transition. The large percentage of students who get lost in the transfer process is a waste of talent and a black-eye to the higher educational systems (Handel, 2007).

The changing American demographic—race, gender, ethnicity—mean that universities and colleges must educate a broader student base; a student base that also has fewer academic and financial resources. Community colleges will not only continue to educate students from groups that have been underrepresented in higher education but will enroll significantly more of them in the future (Handel, 2007).

Fortunately, four year schools are making an effort to make the transition from 2 to 4 year schools easier. In one example, the Jack Kent Cooke Foundation and eight collegiate institutions, including Amherst College and Cornell University, planned to pump millions of dollars into increasing the number of low- and moderate-income community college students who transfer to their school. The Universities of Wisconsin-Madison and Virginia University also made plans to enroll more community-college students. Indeed, several top-notch universities, among them, Harvard, Princeton, and Stanford Universities are interested in the results of how well community-college students fare at a four year schools (Handel, 2007).

Continuing this trend, some of California's four-year institutions are working with community colleges,to assist in the successful transition of students; making it cost-effective and easier for students to cross the bridge between two and four year colleges (Handel, 2007).

The University of California (UC) aims to accept community college students first instead of giving preference to students transferring to UC from another four year college. Without transferring, no community college students can complete a 4 year degree but the University of California argues that transfers from four year schools can at least earn their degree from their native school if they aren't accepted into UC (Handel, 2007).

Some students feel ashamed of going to their local community college because of the stigma it still carries. The widely-held view is that community colleges are just a glorified high school for the dumb and dumber. Nothing could be further from the truth because community colleges can provide skills training and academic challenges that make students more prepared for the rigors of a four-year college. There have been thousands of community college students who've gone on to become teachers, doctors, lawyers, accountants, and engineers.

Besides, a four-year institution my cost $50,000—$200,000 by the time a student graduates. By investing the first two years in a community college and then transferring, students can cut that total cost by 30-40%.

Combating School Violence

"From whence come wars and fightings among you? Come they not hence, even of your lusts that war in your members? Ye lust, and have not, ye kill, and desire to have, and cannot obtain, ye fight and war, yet ye have not, because ye ask not. Ye ask, and receive not, because ye ask amiss, that ye may consume it upon your lusts. Ye adulterers and adulteresses, know ye not that the friendship of the world is enmity with GOD? Whosever therefore will be friend of the world is the enemy of GOD"

James 4:1-4 KJV

One of the best ways to combat school violence is to sell youngsters a hope in their future. Youth are well-positioned to develop strong character, choose skill-appropriate careers, and network for future opportunities

Character Education

Character education in schools is gaining ground nationwide. The growing emphasis on character education in schools which involve "universally accepted values (e.g., love, truthfulness, fairness, tolerance, responsibility) finds little opposition based on differing political, social, and religious beliefs." Thanks to initiatives like this, pregnancy and dropout rates have been cut in half in some schools with large numbers of at-risk children (Stephens, 2007)

Career Exploration

The United States and abroad are full of career opportunities in various fields—including education, business, technology, recreation, human development and performance, military, politics and health. Students have more ways to sell themselves to potential employers than ever before.

Of course there is the standard resume and cover letters that we all do for job applications, but there are other techniques which help position youth into future career options before they even leave high school.

Networking

George Fraser is one of the world's foremost tacticians in professional networking. He gives seminars and training on how to build a network base from scratch. His advice is to make sure you collect business cards, emails, etc. and file them in an organized database of some sort (electronic or handwritten).

Rhoda Smith, a Syracuse University alumnus and native of Toronto, Canada chimes in regarding the importance of youth networking for academic/career opportunities:

"I would advise students to begin building a strong network base. A broad network base can come in very handy when relocating to a new city or state and could be useful when searching for work at a specific company or organization. Sometimes the people you meet along the way can be a good source of referrals and references. It's also very useful to have a combination of faculty, staff, and friends with a wide variety of majors in your network. Students are often reluctant to network with high school teachers and college professors and refuse to get to know some of the administrators.

To enhance their chances of breaking into their chosen career field, I would also advise students to volunteer in their field of interest prior to accepting a job in that field; better to be sure about what you don't want to do instead of taking a job and finding out later its not what you want. Volunteering also gives you a chance to check out a company and learn about advancement possibilities and the work environment from a first hand point of view.

Lastly, I would encourage students to value and maintain friendships made during these formative years. I still have friends from high school and undergrad and to this day these are the people that keep me grounded, sane, and most important help me through tough times and situations."

BRYCE K. BEVILL

"For all that is in the world, the lust of the flesh, and the lust of the eyes, and the pride of life, is not of the Father, but is of the world. And the world passeth away, and the lust thereof, but he that doeth the will of GOD abideth ever"

Jonah 2:16-17 KJV

Glenn Harris has been in the media business for a number of decades in the Washington, D.C. area. Although he has branded himself in the sports reporting arena, Glenn is a very versatile person with an inexhaustible interest in fine arts, culture, research and psychology. Glenn speaks to many parents and youth at receptions, conferences, and banquets about issues relating to their growth and development.

Recently Glenn told a number of athletes and parents to make sure that the young men and women in the audience refrain from becoming near-sighted and narrow-minded in their views. He encouraged them to listen to different types of music and read different genres of books & magazines. In paraphrasing his words, he recommended that they "use their opportunity to gain a quality education to their advantage because their parents and many others fought and died for that opportunity."

He continues to tell audiences wherever he goes that the sensation of violence and thievery keep youth from achieving their full potential. He also asks parents and neighbors to be concerned not only for their child, but their neighbor's child as well.

Spoken like a true villager.

The business of rearing tomorrow's youth today is as challenging and rewarding as ever. It is Bryce K. Bevill's and Roland "Bubba" Grimes' sincere hope that you've read something in these pages that gives you additional insight into youth development and helps you to edify others as we all raise tomorrow's youth, today.

Thank You and GOD Bless.

A SUMMATION
Love and the Fierce Urgency, Yet Fierce Danger of NOW

By Roland "Bubba" Grimes

I watched a movie many years ago called the "Five Heartbeats" with actor/director Robert Townsend. In one very poignant scene, someone told Townsend's character that he probably will be able to write great songs someday... *after he has suffered enough.*

Not only have I told hundreds of young men and women not to wait until they've suffered death, disharmony, divorce, destruction, and betrayal before they decide to do the things necessary to amaze people, I've had to grapple with the same obstacles myself.

Fortunately it has become much easier and simpler for me to work toward greatness everyday instead of waiting for something (or someone) to "bust" me in the chest because I've learned to recognize and respect the POWER of NOW.

However, "now" comes with it a whole lot of baggage. I remember reading excerpts from Martin Luther King's letters from the Birmingham jail as he remarked how so many of his colleagues and contemporaries were mad as hell at him for having the audacity to try to change the culture of the segregated South before it became a universally accepted concept. "Martin, just wait man. People will come around eventually," I'm sure they reasoned with King. What many of them did not understand is that Martin had an overwhelming love for his fellow man. He acted upon his compulsion to "love" with such intensity that the fear and dangers of the "now" paled in comparison.

As much as I like funky music, I admit that one of my favorite tunes is by the incomparable Stephanie Mills called ("I've learned to respect) The POWER of LOVE. Whenever my fears of the "now" creep in, I play that song in my head and I drive on.

The Turning Point

I truly believe that GOD warns me beforehand when HE wants me to act on the "now." Many times, it is something I've read or heard, or observed that compels me to take extra action. Recently GOD used two people whom I love dearly to flash light on the "now" for me. They are Syracuse Orange basketball and football alumni **"Fast" Eddie Moss** and **"Go-Go" Walter Moseley**.

Eddie was a point guard and Walter was a tailback for the Orange's basketball and football teams respectively. In high school, my coaches Rohan, McNamara, and Neitzey taught me as an offensive lineman and fullback that my responsibility was to love and protect my quarterbacks and tailbacks: UNCONDITIONALLY.

In junior high school, my basketball coaches, Allen and Henshaw taught me to love and protect my point guards. My being the coach-able diehard soldier that I was back then, I developed an unwavering regard for my high school QB's and TB's and if anyone encounters said persons by the names of Rohan, Disbennett, Piazza, Horne, Klein, V. McPherson,

Hunter, Greg Smith or Todd Bozeman please let them know that my coaches also explained to me that this was not just a player commitment. It is a "life" commitment.

If someone out there meets former Syracuse University tailbacks or quarterbacks by the names of Gayden, Abraham, Drummond, Carter, Moore, Covington or L. Morris, Norley, Christodulu, Kmetz, D. McPherson, or Philcox, the same courtesy is afforded them as well. My Syracuse point guards during my tenure were Gene Waldron, "Pearl" Washington and Sherman Douglas. My love and protection for former Orange basketball player Howard Triche who was not a point guard there goes even deeper and broader than my love for even some of my football teammates.

Along the way, I also vicariously adopted a few Orange QB's and TB's and point guards who played after I graduated by the names of Owens, McNabb (yes *the* McNabb), Autry, Hart, Walker, Richardson, and of course Sherman Douglas, Marvin Graves, and Lawrence Moten from the Chocolate City. Bruce Bevill lined up as a tailback for a brief cup of coffee and that was long enough for me.

My coaches also taught me to extend the same "life" commitment to my teachers, employers, alma maters and get this one: *Former girlfriends who put up with my stupidity.*

I "now" understand why my coaches taught me to love and protect those whom I serve because Walter Moseley and Eddie Moss gave me two gifts that keep on giving. They knew that I would never intentionally hurt them or quit them. It was Walter who told me a decade ago that he was enrolled in a graduate program at Syracuse University's School of Education that would allow him to earn *two* Masters in Counselor Education. He admitted that some of life's issues were gnawing at his energy and he was having trouble finishing the program but he wanted me to consider enrolling in it too (which my beloved wife had 'bust" me in my chest over for many months before...(she can do that but if the rest of y'all dream about doing it you'd better wake up to apologize).

After finishing the program I ran into Walter and as is my custom with my TB's and QB's, and point guards, I hugged him and kissed him and thanked him. He said that he hoped to return to finish his program someday.

The gift that Eddie Moss gave me that keeps on giving is he begged and pleaded with me to leave the City of Syracuse and return to my native DC or somewhere within 300 miles *South* of the place. He told me that if I was anywhere North of it he'd "bust" me in my chest. Low and behold, my wife had compelled me to do the same thing for 10 years of our marriage.

GOD sent me a tailback and a point guard to entrench the things that my wife had been telling me for years but I just didn't recognize and respect the "fierce urgency of the now." My wife planted those seeds, Walt and Eddie watered them, and GOD gave them the increase.

Flash Light on Me

I did not recognize the "urgency of the now" but I quickly understood the "dangers of the now" when it came to getting a Masters degree or relocating to the Chocolate City.

One of my first stops when I came home was to a place my family affectionately calls "eleven-oh-five" where my beloved Uncle Allen sat with me for hours one night and shared his stories and thoughts. Since I was a young boy, I loved to sit and listen to older men and women tell me those stories. Uncle

Allen told me that he was happy to see me return but sad at the same time. He told me that DC had changed so much since I left that it was "now" a dangerous social and political place like never before. He told me that I would not be able to freely move about socially or professionally "now" because the soul that was the "Chocolate City" had been sucked out by the trickery, greed, and deceit of the human mind and heart. "It's a shame," he said, "that our desires for making ourselves better and wealthier put more hatred into our hearts and soul. We should never have played it this way. Bubba, I fear for you."

Whoa!!! This dude is a celebrated Vietnam War veteran who I expected to be the last one, not the first one, to tell me about the "fierce danger of now" here in my native land. If there was any doubt in mind about the "danger" of returning to DC to live, work, and grow, Uncle Allen put that to rest. Thanks Unc!

On the other hand, I understood beyond a shadow of doubt about the "danger" of my earning an advanced degree.

One of my college professors "Rick" Wright was the one guy that the Syracuse football coaches wanted the black recruits to meet during the Dick MacPherson coaching era. Dr. Wright was a "trip" and he could entertain a graveyard. He was the first to inform me that large, dark-skinned, articulate African-American male football players were very limited in their career choices. He told me that I needed to get advanced degrees but not to expect a lot of pats on the back when I got my Masters and Doctorate.

Many of the black male administrators and professors at Syracuse University reminded me that I was a "threat" to nearly every establishment because I did not fear the work it took to be great. They assured me that I was too big, too black, and too smart for my own good. However, each of them offered me support and resources because they also understood that there was not a drop of larceny in my heart. They realized that my compassion for doing great things was fueled by my love for others and not my own aggrandizement. I only put myself out there because I had the will and might to do it for the benefit of others...and the detriment of myself.

As Larry Martin at the Program Development Office (Syracuse University) told me when I called to tell him I was moving back home, *"I will admit that we are losing a prize in you. You tried to get us to increase our social, political, athletic and academic potential on this campus and in this city; and you did it despite the fact that the few of us who did come along sometimes were kicking and screaming every step of the way. Roland you made a lot of sense, but many of us were too uncomfortable to listen."*

It was at that moment in conversation with Larry that I realized that if a college campus for all of its experimentation and cutting-edge risk and reward, was ambivalent or unwilling to accept renaissance from a guy like me whom they *trained* to be that way, no matter where I landed, foxes would have holes and birds would have nests, but *I* was going to be one lonely dude.

But even if there was a shadow of doubt in mind, the day I woke up with tears in my eyes realizing that I "now" had to **remove the mention of football** from my resume was confirmation of the "danger of now" in a guy like me getting advanced degrees.

As I told my wife and Walter on separate occasions, the quickest way for me to become completely unemployable was to get a Masters Degree. I'd always kept football on my resume but would frequently omit the Masters Degree and "water down" my skills and training. GOD's word, I believe in the book of James, says, "Be not many masters because in many things you offend all." I knew that my resume with all of my training and skills would get me in the door to an interview. I learned, like most of you, the objective is to get in the door, right?

In my experience, as soon as most employers opened the door their smiling faces turned upside down as soon as they took one look at me; thinking to themselves they must have somehow mixed up the applications. My only response was to sadly accept the fact that I could not give the teachers, coaches, parents/siblings, neighbors, ministers, teammates, extended family, friends and girlfriends who helped shape me the acknowledgment they were due by reflecting their influence in my resume because it would not help me to feed my children.

Be not deceived, it was not as much a race issue, as it was a "perception" issue. Employers and college admissions departments have preconceived notions about the value of your experience before you even walk in the door. I quickly learned not to express the breadth and depth of my training and skills because most people could not conceptualize that a guy like me could possible be that versatile unless I cheated or lied. Many would automatically think that somehow I cut corners as a student or stole time from my employer because I could not possibly be either that intelligent or disciplined to walk and chew chewing gum at the same time.

Little do they know that in high school and semi-pro football, I learned the techniques and intricacies to play every position on the offensive line, every position on the defensive line, fullback, tailback, tight end, kickoff returner and outside linebacker *within the same football season*...and performed respectively in each role within a moments' notice under extreme environmental pressure (playing against DeMatha and

Archbishop Carroll was as close to true warfare as I'd ever want to get).

Anyone who knows football will tell you that it takes much more than a talented athlete to play that many positions at the same time. The body that is used by a coach to play outside linebacker is not the same body that plays center and noseguard; the body that is good at center is definitely not the same body that plays tailback. **Quite frankly, no coach in his right mind would ever make an offensive tackle their *kickoff returner*…**but eventually, mine did.

Anyone who knows football knows that it is geometrically impossible for one player to play that many diametrically opposite positions on a football field *at any level*. True, physically it is impossible. **Mentally and spiritually, *impossible is nothing*.**

Nonetheless, I know that many people could not possibly bend their minds around the fact that a guy like me could be so versatile so I removed much of my experiences and training from my resume. It was when I had to remove football from my resume that My Uncle's advice hit home.

Why "Now" Bubba?

Many people can't remember, or just don't want to remember, the time when the very same people who uphold Martin Luther King as a great American now, simply loathed him as Martin "Lucifer Koon" many years ago. A few decades ago, Bobby Kennedy was not necessarily a favorite of the American aristocrat or proletariat. Malcolm X was once considered Public Enemy #1.

People aren't always going to like you or like what you do. For many years, I allowed my desire to be liked by others, not the inherent "dangers of now," to obstruct my calling to respond to the "urgency of now."

Walter Moseley's encouragement to get me over the hump to get a Masters degree helped me to accept the fact that friends or family, or teammates could become jealous and standoffish. He helped me to come to grips with the fact that my employment options would become limited because people wouldn't want someone with a Masters degree to haul trash or shovel poop. In other words, he helped me to accept the reality that there were millions of lower-level jobs for millions of people who needed to work, but there were far fewer higher-level jobs for brothers like us to access. People wouldn't mind seeing brothers like us shoveling poop or working on their staff, but would have much more difficulty seeing us in the corner office in a suit and tie; thereby limiting our employment options. We knew that America talked that stuff about seeing brothers emerge to a higher plain but was far more accustomed to seeing brothers in orange jumpsuits, in football helmets, in basketball shorts, or singing and dancing on stage.

Walter also reminded me in his own words, "Bubba the scary thing about it is that you are strong enough to dig ditches, trained enough to manage a company, poetic enough to play hoops, fierce enough to play football, and funky enough to take the stage. Don't be too scared to get your Masters degree and represent it for the whole world to see. As you know, your wife is right."

Eddie Moss had moved to North Carolina and continued to build on the Black newspaper I had the privilege of working on with him a few times in Syracuse. Eddie was less apologetic than Walter, "Ro man, time to go. I found some jobs where brothers as big and black as you are working and folks ain't nearly as scared as what we are used to seeing. Get your family, let's go. Down here, you don't have to worry too much about white people trying to hurt you. Down here, Blacks are very able and all too willing to kill ourselves. A brotha like you can flash light and cut through some of that with your writing alone; so let's make it happen."

And then he dropped the bomb on me…"**But Ro, don't you put *football* on your resume. It'll hurt you.**"

Football was such a powerful gift from GOD to me that I just couldn't understand why it had such negative interpretation to so many people in society. I believed (as Uncle Allen would say, "Bubba are you going to be simple all of your life?) if I conducted myself as a gentleman and worked hard in school, served my community, respected women, and demonstrated a love for the word of GOD that people would come to realize by my living example that football players are only as dumb and limited as the grown folks around them make them to be. It's not the athletes themselves who *chose* not to **learn** to conjugate a verb while rescuing the dangling participle, calculate pie, examine the effects of the trickle down theory, network the LAN & WAN, juxtapose the interior/exterior of architectural design, or articulate the interdependence of atmospheric-geographic-oceanographic forces on climate. *It wasn't us who made the fuss.*

It was the grown folks around us in the school, at home, and in the neighborhood, who upon discovering that we could wiggle our hips, run faster than a speeding bullet, halt a powerful locomotive and leap tall buildings in a single bound discouraged us from putting our time & energy into the *learning* and put it more into the *playing*. It was the grown folks around us who told us that if we wanted it bad enough that we had to give our all to eating right, running and lifting weights, studying film and play, play and play some more if we wanted be great in sports. Somewhere along the way, we grown folks encouraged youth to put 75% of their discretionary time into getting better on the field or court, or track and leave the remaining 25% for family, friends, recreation, and… oops…*studying*. The adult byline that was passed down from generation to generation is, "just get your homework done."

Flash light: **Just getting homework done is just not enough. If we'd put half as much time in studying as we did preparing for a sport, we would all be world-renowned brain surgeons today.**

It's not the athlete's fault. The kids are getting screwed and it's us adults who are screwing them. But even my real-life example has not been enough to enlighten other people about the worth to society of someone as low-class as a football player. I thought my biggest hump in professional circles would be my skin color. Lord was I ever wrong about that one.

So I took football off of my resume. Every time I take something off my resume that I am proud of, I find myself writing about it in a different venue to maintain my self-dignity and sanity.

"Now" you are going to read the next book: ***"DIVISION ONE IS NO GAME."*** *Now* you are going to read about the "bookends" of McNamara who helped transform the way a high school thought about football and its football players. So much so, that one college coach today says that he decided he wanted to train-up young men the rest of his life after spending one season coaching "the bookends."

"Now" you are going to read the good, the bad, and the ugly of big-time ball from the mouths of those who've played

and coached it firsthand instead of just hearing it from the armchair quarterbacks and couch-potato point guards who never played the game but talk like they are experts because they have a microphone and a pen.

The "fierce urgency of now" and the "fierce danger of now" go hand in hand.

There is a hook-line in the song "Funkin' For Fun" by Parliament in the Clones of Dr. Funkenstein album (my big sister's all-time favorite album). The line goes:

"If you see my mother, tell her I'm alright. If you get a chance to see my father, my brother, tell them that everything's alright. I'm just funkin' around for fun."

—Parliament, 1976

There was a Syracuse football player from Archbishop Carroll High School in Washington DC who'd graduated and was moving back home for good my freshman year at the 'Cuse. Before he left, I asked him to see my mother (whom he'd never met) and tell her that although I was homesick and cried a lot (and ran up her phone bill), I was alright...soon I'd be a real Orangeman and would be funkin' around here for fun. I just needed to get over the hump and get over myself because I found out that Division One football was no game. He did me that favor and twenty-plus years later he is still married to my big sister (I guess fantasy is reality, eh sis?)

The gentleman who sang that song for Parliament is the voice that keeps on giving to my family, friends, and the Chocolate City. Glenn Goins has the most "churchified" voice you have ever heard (Tom Vickers), and he could make 20,000 screaming people cry at a "P-Funk" concert. He sang two songs that lifted me up from every down I knew. One song was called "Endangered Species" and the other was "Funkin' For Fun."

Just like Walter Moseley and Eddie Moss, Glenn Goins' words (out of Plainfield, NJ) inspired me to accept and overcome the "fierce urgency and fierce danger of now" as you land the Mothership long before the masses can understand. But I've learned and Bevill and others have joined in despite their fears and trepidation (of course a 400 pound brother named Bubba leaning on you everyday is also great motivation).

The hardest hump to get over is that the Mothership travels in two directions: It comes **Down** to get you and goes **Up** to take you away.

So I'm praying to my grandmothers, my grandfathers, my nephew Zaccheus, my Aunt Ann, and father-figure Jim Jackson and many others to tell Glenn Goins for me that he inspired me to get over the hump.

See, one of the revelations of the "fierce urgency and danger of now" is that we never know when "now" is no longer available to us. I'm praying that these family members will pass the word to Glenn because I can no longer ask them in person. They, like Glenn have board the Mothership for the final time.

As well I'm asking them to tell Walter and Eddie that I love them and give them a hug and kiss for me as is my custom. I can't love and protect my tailback and point guard anymore.

Eddie doesn't know I'm home.

He and Walter left too.

A SUMMATION
Bryce Pays Price Twice

By Bryce Bevill

Many college and professional athletes understand all too well that in this life we pay the price twice to be able to compete in sports at the highest levels: One price on the way up, and another price on the way down.

First, I'd like to thank GOD for all of the trials that he has brought me through because without GOD none of this is possible.

In order for me to advance and excel as a student-athlete, I knew I needed to adjust my way of thinking and doing. I realized that I had to pay a price in order to raise my level of performance in and out of the classroom.

It started for me the moment I walked on Syracuse University's campus to play football for the Orange. Knowing the stereotypes that are associated with football players, I wanted to separate myself from that culture. What was that culture like? Pretty much the same way it is now: Isolated, Impenetrable, Ignorant.

I began to change by placing restrictions on myself (self-restraint). I would 1) never to go out to clubs during the week, 2) attend all classes during my freshman year and 3) abstain from drinking or smoking. The main one: 4) Do No Drugs of any kind.

However, the change that made the greatest impact on my life then and now was 5) to never, ever allow anyone "out-work me." Those were the basic principles that carried me through college. I shared it with others but not many took to it.

Karlos Jackson was a player that I enjoyed playing with and even admired. We both graduated from DeMatha. We lost the championship our senior year to a St. John's team that was anchored by none other than the founder of "Under Armour" himself, former University of Maryland football player Kevin Plank (www.underarmour.com).

Karlos and I had seen each others' best and worst. Karlos was the best athlete that I have ever seen; with GOD given ability that put most of us to shame. Bubba invited Karlos to play in an alumni basketball game in 1995 and they raised the basket to 11 feet just to make the game interesting. Karlos was the only former Orange football player who actually leaped high enough to slam the ball. He was going to have his ticket punched to the NFL. I wanted to be there with him. So I went to work. With my five rules of self-management to follow in college, I didn't have time for friends.

My position coach Phil Elmmassion taught me how to play the defensive back position from a mental standpoint. Under his tutelage, the prospect of playing in the NFL became real to me. In college is where I realized that it takes a very special human being to play high-level football. It is completely unnatural and somewhat psychotic to run full speed into another human being on purpose. I learned from Science class that two objects (mass) cannot occupy the same space at the same time. Therefore, mass plus acceleration equals force. If I worked hard enough to strengthen my body and improve my speed, I could excel in college and move on to the pros.

Coach Kevin Coyle was my defensive coach who gave me the confidence that I could actually make it in the NFL. Armed with my five principles, I didn't engage many of my college school-mates because my teammates and I spent so much time together. I had a few non-football friends and that was about all I could handle with the pressures and demands of Division One football.

Many college and professional athletes understand all too well that in this life we pay the price twice to be able to compete in sports at the highest levels: One price on the way up, and another price on the way down.

Eventually, I arrived at an NFL camp in Detroit Michigan but was summarily dismissed from the Lions. That year, my first daughter, Adayre, was born. I was a new father with no job and a college degree with no real-world work experience or skills.

I took my medicine from being cut by the Lions and worked out even harder and more determined than ever. I trusted in GOD that everything would work out for the best. It did, and I signed a two year contract with the CFL Saskatchwan RoughRiders. Things were getting good again as I was getting paid to play football. To survive in the CFL, I went back to my five basic principles. But after playing in the championship Grey Cup game, I was released from the RoughRiders and claimed by the Winnipeg Blue Bombers.

Shortly after, I was called by an NFL team who wanted to sign me as a free agent. I felt like I'd finally come full circle. My second chance dream was right in my grasp but there was a major hurdle standing in the way: I was under contract with the CFL.

Surely these good folks in Canada would understand that it was the right thing to do by letting me go pursue my dreams to play in the NFL. Surely they did not. As I reported to and worked out in the Winnipeg camp, they cut me after the NFL team had finalized their season's roster; leaving no room for me to sign with them. Suddenly it dawned on a brotha, "Something I had prepared my entire life for was gone and I had no more options to pursue my goal." At 26 my lifelong career had ended when everyone else was just starting theirs. Then the Lord went to work. This is when I began to pay the second price.

Karlos, the football player that I admired the most was kicked out of school before our senior season. He went to a nearby college and received his degree in communication. We still kept in contact when we left Syracuse. Karlos had joined the Army and was off to the Middle East as a bomb specialist. He once told me that no man should experience what he experienced over in the Middle East: "Bryce, no man should see what I've seen." Three years later he was honorably discharged from the Army. But it took its toll and not long after, Karlos took that final ride on the Mothership just like Bubba's boys Eddie and Walter.

As time passed, I truly found out what I was placed on earth to do, and no one, anywhere is going to stop me from fulfilling it; by any means necessary. I started teaching second and third grade at a small catholic school in Washington DC. I also went back to DeMatha and learned coaching under Bill McGregor and Deno Campell. I married and had my second daughter, Jerah and we lived happily ever after...or not. My wife and I were living separate lives as I sought to figure myself out after competing 20 years as an athlete. Eventually, we divorced less than two years of being away from my children.

Teaching and Coaching was where I found my calling. I learned a lot and patterned a lot of my coaching style from the coaches that I'd encountered over the years, including Kevin

Coyle, Phil Elmassion, Paul Pasqualoni, Charlie West, and Bill McGregor. The one coach that I learned perhaps the most from was Deno Campbell.

Throughout my coaching career I have worked with many beautiful young men. When I became the Head Coach at Bishop McNamara I learned that there was an even greater cause than coaching football. I learned, for the first time in life, that football was a vehicle to help young men become real men. Raising young men to become real men is the most important endeavor in the world to me next to being a father to my own children. I found out IT IS NOT ABOUT FOOTBALL.

I started the **TOTAL FOCUS** as my contribution to provide guidance and direction to not only young men playing football, but to young boys and girls aspiring to do anything worthwhile in society.

One of my students recently handed me a quote she picked up from one of the many superlative teachers at McNamara High that sums it all up in one sentence. She said it is taken from a brilliant American man named Frederick Douglas. It reads:

"It is easier to build strong children than to repair broken men."

REFERENCE PAGES

Austin, J., Johnson, K. D., & Gregoriou, M. (2000). Juveniles in adult prisons and jails: A national assessment. Washington, DC: Office of Justice Programs.

Baker, M. L., Sigmon, J. N., & Nugent, M. E. (2001). Truancy reduction: Keeping students in school. Juvenile Justice Bulletin, NCJ-188947, 1-14.

Barton-Arwood, Sally; Jolivette, Kristine; Massey, N Gayle (2000, September). Mentoring with elementary-age students. Intervention in School & Clinic, 36 (1), 36.

Bempechat, Janine (2004, July). The Motivational Benefits of Homework: A Social-Cognitive Perspective. Theory into Practice, 43(3), 189.

Binder, A. (1988). Juvenile delinquency. Annual Review of Psychology, 39, 253-282.

Bishop, D., & Frazier, C. (2000). Consequences of transfer. In J. Pagan & F. Zimring (Eds.), The changing borders of juvenile justice (pp. 227-276). Chicago: University of Chicago Press.

Bishop, John H; Bishop, Matthew; Bishop, Michael; Gelbwasser, Lara; Et al (2004, September). Why We Harass Nerds and Freaks: A Formal Theory of Student Culture and Norms. The Journal of School Health.

Blaylock, T. Herndon; Newman, Joseph W. (2005, April). THE IMPACT OF COMPUTER-BASED SECONDARY EDUATION. Education, 125 (3), 373.

Bohanon, Hank; Fenning, Pamela; Carney, Kelly L; Minnis-Kim, Myoung Jinnie; Et al (206, July). Schoolwide Application of Positive Behavior Support in an Urban High School: A Case Study. Journal of Positive Behavior Interventions.

Callicott, Kimberly J; Park, Hija (2003, November). Effects of Self-Talk on Academic Engagement and Academic Responding. Behavioral Disorders, 29(1).

Campbell, Eleanor T (2005, July). Child Abuse Recognition, Reporting and Prevention: A Culturally Congruent Approach. Journal of Multicultural Nursing & Health, (11)2.

Christner, Terry (2003, October). Brown v. Board of Education: Caste, Culture, and the Constitution. Library Journal, 128 (17), 78.

Chromey, Rick (2006, January). The ABCs of spiritual growth. Group.

Connor, Bill; Mann, David; Sparks, Autumn; Crawford, Scott A G M; Et al (2004, April). Should schools hire park and recreation professionals to serve as resource specialists, as proposed in "Thinking Outside...Journal of Physical Education, Recreation & Dance

Cummings, Merrilyn N (2005, November). Mentoring: A Bridge to the Future of Family and Consumer Sciences. Journal of Family and Consumer, 97 (4), 8.

Davis, Michelle R (2007, February). Gender Gap in GPAs Seen as Linked to Self-Discipline. Education Week, 26(23).

Dilulio, J. (1987). Governing prisons: A comparative study of correctional management. New York: Free Press.

DiIulio, John J Jr (2002, October). The three faith factors. Public Interest.

Drakeford, William; Staples, Jeanine M (2006, September). Minority Confinement in the Juvenile Justice System: Legal, Social, and Racial Factors. Teaching Exceptional Children, 39 (1), 52.

Dudley, Bruce S.; Johnson, David W.; Johnson, Roger (1997, August). Using cooperative learning to enhance the academic and social experiences of freshman student athletes. The Journal of Social Psychology.

Dukes, Howard, **The Word on Karate**, South Bend Tribune, November, 2007.

Edelman, M. W. (1995, Spring). United we stand: A common vision. Claiming Children, 1, 6-12

Foster, E Michael; Jones, Damon E; Bierman, Karen L; Coie, John D; Et al (2005, October). The High Costs of Aggression: Public Expenditures Resulting From Conduct Disorder. American Journal of Public Health, 95 (10), 1767.

Freeman, Gregory D.; Sullivan, Kathleen; Fulton, C. Ray; Effects of creative drama on self-concept, social skills, and problem behavior. The Journal of Educational Research, 96(3).

Freeman, Mike, *Jim Brown: The Fierce Life of an American Hero.* HarperCollns Publishers, New York, NY, 2006.

Fries-Britt, Sharon & Griffin, Kimberly A (2007, September). The Black Box: How High-Achieving Blacks Resist Stereotypes About Black Americans. Journal of College Student Development 48 (5), 509

Furtado, Peter (2004, August). Bridge That Gap. History Today, 54 (8), 2.

Gable, Robert A; Bullock, Lyndal M; Evans, William H (2006, October). Changing Perspectives on Alternative Schooling for Children and Adolescents With Challenging Behavior. Preventing School Failure.

Gilbert, Jenelle N; Gilbert, Wade; Morawski, Cynthia (2007, February). Coaching Strategies for Helping Adolescent Athletes Cope with Stress. Journal of Physical Education, Recreation & Dance, 78 (2), 13

Gilroy, Marilyn (2003, March). Articulating the K-16 dream. The Education Digest, 68 (7), 19.

Giroux, Henry A (2001, November). Zero Tolerance, Domestic Militarization, and the War Against Youth. Social Justice, 30 (2), 59.

Granello, Paul F; Hanna, Fred J (2003, January). Incarcerated and court-involved adolescents: Counseling an at-risk population. Journal of Counseling and Development, 81 (1), 11.

Grimes, Roland Bubba, America's Legacy: The Economic Subordination of African-Descendants, Hispanics & Women. Trafford Publishing, 2004.

Graham, A. Lee / Staff Writer of The Dallas Morning News, Mentoring program aids at-risk H-E-B Students. The Arlington Morning News December 5, 1998

Gullat, D. E., & Lemoine, D. A. (1997). The school truancy dilemma. Retrieved February 15, 2003, from http://www.edrs.com

Handel, Stephen J. (2007, September). SECOND CHANCE, Not Second Class: A Blueprint for Community-College Transfer. Change, 39 (5), 38).

Hanna, F. J., Hanna, C. A., & Keys, S. G. (1999). Fifty strategies for counseling defiant, aggressive, adolescents: Reaching, accepting, and relating. Journal of Counseling & Development, 77, 395-404.

Harrison, C Keith; Comeaux, Eddie; Plecha, Michelle (2006, June). Faculty and Male Football and Basketball Players on University Campuses: An Empirical Investigation of the "Intellectual." Research Quarterly for Exercise and Sport, 77 (2), 277

Harvey, Aminifu R; Hill, Robert B (2004, January). Africentric Youth and Family Rites of Passage Program: Promoting Resilience among At-Risk African American Youths. Social Work.

Heiberg, Jeanne (2006, February). Help Your Students See Themselves. Catechist, (39) 5.

http://www.finalcall.com/artman/publish/article_3018.shtml.

http://www.soulofsyracuse.com, Nov. 2007

Irvin, Judith L (1996, March). Developmental tasks of early adolescence: how adult awareness can reduce at-risk behavior.(Special Section: Young Adolescents At Risk). The Clearing House.

Johnson, Eric, How to Live with Parents & Teachers. The Westminster Press, Philadelphia, Pa., 1986.

Johnson-Siebold, Judith (2005, October). Living by the Word. The Christian Century, 122 (20).

Journal of Physical Education, Anonymous 2007

Juby, Heather; Bourdais, Celine Le; Marcil-Gratton (2005, February). Sharing Roles, Sharing Custody? Couples' Characteristics and Children's Living Arrangements at Separation. Journal of Marriage and the Family

Kaplan, Leslie S., **Coping with Peer Pressure.**The Rosen Publishing Group, New York, 1993.

Kat, James (2006, September). Saving Yourself from Compulsive Self-Sabotage. Total Health, 28(3).

Kaufman, David M (2003, January). Applying educational theory in practice; British Medical Journal (International edition).

Keating, Lisa M; Tomishima, Michelle A; Foster, Sharon; Alessandri, Michael (2002, January). The effects of mentoring program on at-risk youth. Adolescence, 37 (148), 717.

Keyser, Tom; KARATE and kindness ; Before these students learn to punch, they first offer a helping hand; Staff Writer, Times Union (Albany), September 2007.

Koblinsky, Sally A; Kuvalanka, Katherine A; McClintock-Comeaux, Marta (2006, January). Preparing Future Faculty and Family Professionals. Family Relations, 55 (1), 29.

Kogan, Rick, As neighborhoods change, small urban churches find a way to survive. Chicago Tribune Knight-Ridder/Tribune News Service, June 2006.

Kuhn, Deanna (2007). How to Produce A High-Achieving Child. Phi Delta Kappa.

Kupchik, Aaron (2007, June). The Correctional Experiences of Youth in Adult and Juvenile Prisons. Justice Quarterly, 24 (2), 247.

Kupchik, A. (2003). Prosecuting adolescents in criminal courts: Criminal or juvenile justice? Social Problems, 50, 439-460.

Kupchik, A. (2004). Youthfulness, responsibility and punishment: Admonishing adolescents in criminal court. Punishment and Society, 6, 149-173.

Kupchik, A. (2006). Judging juveniles: Prosecuting adolescents in adult and juvenile courts. New York: New York University Press.

Lee, Janet (1997)

Lee, Suk-Hyang; Theoharis, Raschelle; Fitzpatrick, Michael; Kim, Kyeong-Hwa; Et al (2006, March). Create Effective Mentoring Relationships: Strategies for Mentor and Mentee Success. Intervention in School & Clinic, 41 (4).

Leffert, N., P. L. Benson, PC. Scales, A. Sharma, D. Drake, and D. A. Blyth. 1998. Developmental assets: Measurement and prediction of risk behaviors among adolescents. Applied Developmental Science 2(4): 209-30

Leon, Kim (2003, July). Risk and protective factors in young children's adjustment to parental divorce: A review of the research. Family Relations, 52 (3).

Linek, Wayne M.: Fleener, Charlene; Fazio, Michelle; Raine, I LaVerne; Klakamp, Kimberly (2003, November). The Impact of Shifting From "How Teachers Teach " to "How Children Learn." The Journal of Education Research, 97(2).

Longman & Zack 2003

Mangold, William D; Bean, Luann; Adams, Douglas (2003, September). The impact of intercollegiate athletics on graduation rates among major NCAA Division I universities: Implications for…The Journal of Higher Education, 74 (5).

McCray, Erica D (2006). It's 10 a.m: Do You Know Where Your Children Are? Intervention in School & Clinic, 42 (1), 30.

McCreary, M.; Wright, R (1997, Spring). Effects of Negative Stereotypes on African American Male and Female Relationships. Journal of African American Men, (2)4.

McCurdy, Barry L; Mannella, Mark C; Eldridge, Norris (2003, July). Positive behavior support in urban schools: Can we prevent the escalation of antisocial behavior? Journal of Positive Behavior Interventions, 5 (3), 158.

Medina, Monica A.; Morrone, Anastasia S.; Anderson, Jeffrey A. (2005, May). Promoting Social Justice in an Urban Secondary Teacher Education Program. The Clearing House, 78 (5), 207.

Morse, Jennifer Roback (2003, August). Parents or prisons. Policy Review, 50 (5), 58.

Murray, Steven R; Lasman, Lance J; Lierman, Andy; Docheff, Dennis; Et al (2002, April). Should commercial sponsorship be used to subsidize athletics programs? Journal of Physical Education, Recreation & Dance, 73(4), 9.

National Institute of Corrections. (1995). Offenders under age 18 in state adult correctional systems: A national picture. Longmont, CO: National Institute of Corrections Information Center.

Peterson, Reece L; Skiba, Russell (2001, July). Creating school climates that prevent school violence. Journal of Social Studies Research, 92 (4).

Raby, Rebecca (2005, February). Polite, Well-dressed and on Time: Secondary School Conduct Codes and the Production of Docile Citizens*; The Canadian Review of Sociology and Anthropology, 42 (1).

Resnick, Paul; Brice, Jeff; Christie, Bryan; Christiansen, Jennifer C. Filtering (1997, March) Information on the Internet. Scientific American. 03-01-1997

Rimm-Kaufman, Sara E; Voorhees, Mary D; Snell, Martha E; Paro, Karen M La (2003, October). Improving the sensitivity and responsivity of preservice teachers toward young children with disabilities. Topics in Early Childhood Special Education, 23 (3).

Sabia, Joseph J (2007, October) READING, WRITING, AND SEX: THE EFFECT OF LOSING VIRGINITY ON ACADEMIC PERFORMANCE. *Economic Inquiry*

Scales, Peter C (2000, November). Building students' developmental assets to promote health and school success. The Clearing House, 74 (2), 84.

Schilling, Tammy A (2001, December). An investigation on commitment among participants in an extended day physical activity program. Research Quarterly for Exercise and Sport.

Schwimmer, J. B., Burwinkle, T. M., & Varni, J. W. (2003) Health-related quality of life of severely obese children and adolescents, lournal of the American Medical Association, 289, 1813-1819

Skiba, R. J., Peterson, R. L., & Williams, T. (1997). Office referrals and suspension: Disciplinary intervention in middle schools. Education & Treatment of Children, 20, 295-316.

Smith, B. (1998). Children in custody: 20-year trends in juvenile detention, correctional, and shelter facilities. Crime and Delinquency, 44, 526-543.

Smith, Anne; Kozleski, Elizabeth B (2005, September). Witnessing Brown: Pursuit of an Equity Agenda in American Education. Remedial & Special Education, 26 (5), 270.

Smith, B. (1998). Children in custody: 20-year trends in juvenile detention, correctional, and shelter facilities. Crime and Delinquency, 44, 526-543.

Sobolewski, Juliana M; Amato, Paul R (2007, March). Parents' Discord and Divorce, Parent-Child Relationships and Subjective Well-Being in Early Adulthood: Is Feeling Close. Social Forces, 85 (3), 1105.

Stanley, Christine (2007, January). Using Focus Groups to Explore the Stressful Life Events of Black College Men. Journal of College Student Development, 48 (1), 105.

Stein, Nancy; Katz, Susan Roberta; Madriz, Ester; Shick, Shelley (1997, January) Losing a generation: Probing the myths and realities of youth and violence. Social Justice, 24 (4), 1.

Stephens, Gene (1997, March). Youth at Risk: Saving the World's Most Precious Resource. The Futurist

Strickland, V. P. (1999). Attendance and grade point average: A study. Retrieved November 13, 2003, from http://www.edrs.com

Stewart, Craig; Warhol, John; Overton, Kim; Wiet, Chad E; Et al (2005, January). Issues: Has the decline of intramural sports contributed to the youth obesity epidemic? Journal of Physical Education, Recreation & Dance, 76 (1), 11.

Stodghill, Ron/Chicago (2005, October). Soul on Ice Jeffrey Hood was headed for a life of crime—until a church-going business owner unfroze the young man's potential. FSB Fortune Small Business, 15 (8).

Snyder, H., & Sickmund, M. (1999). Juvenile offenders and victims: A national report. National Center for Juvenile Justice.

Terzian, Sevan G (2004, October). The Elusive Goal of School Spirit in the Comprehensive High School: A Case History, 1916-1941. The High School, 88 (1), 42.

Thompson, LaTasha R; Lewis, Bradford F (2005, April) Shooting for the Stars: A Case Study of the Mathematics Achievement and Career Attainment of an African American Male…The High School Journal.

Tuzzolo, Ellen; Hewitt, Damon T (2006, December). Rebuilding Inequity The Re-emergence of the School-to-Prison Pipeline in New Orleans. The High School Journal.

Van Staveren, Tonia; Dale, Darren (2004). Childhood Obesity: PROBLEMS AND SOLUTIONS. Journal of Physical Education & Recreation.

Wagner, Jodie, Studio wants Young Students to Apply Martial Arts lessons Outside classroom. The Palm Beach Post, January 19, 2007.

Walker, H. M., Colvin, G., & Ramsey, E. (1995). Antisocial behavior in school: Strategies and best practices. Pacific Grove, CA:
Brooks/Cole.

Webber, Jo Watkins, Daphne C; Green, B Lee; Goodson, Patricia; Guidry, Jeff. (1997, March). Comprehending Youth Violence: A Practicable Perspective. Remedial & Special Education.

Wilson, J., & Howell, J. (1993). A comprehensive strategy for serious, violent, and chronic juvenile offenders. Washington, DC: U.S. Department of Justice, Office of Juvenile Justice and Delinquency Prevention.

Wolniak, Gregory C; Pierson, Christopher T; Pascarella, Ernest T (2001, November). Effects of intercollegiate athletic participation on male orientations toward learning. Journal of College Student Development, 42 (6), 604.

Wright, R; McCreary, M (1997, Summer). The Talented Ten: Supporting African American Male College Students. Journal of African American Men, (3)1.

Zinsser, Nathaniel; Perkins, Larry D; Gervais, Pierre D; Burbelo, Gregory A (2004, September). Military Application of Performance-Enhancement Psychology. Military Review, 84 (5).

Made in the USA